THE 1967 BELVIDERE TORNADO

MIKE DOYLE

THE History PRESS

Published by The History Press
Charleston, SC
www.historypress.net

First published 2017

Manufactured in the United States

ISBN 9781467136167

Library of Congress Control Number: 2016956924

This book is dedicated to all who live in Boone County. We have the resilience to overcome adversity, the awareness of local traditions and the compassion to help when needed. And to Micah, Will, Molly and Sam.

CONTENTS

Foreword, by Jerry Rowe 7
Preface 9
Acknowledgements 11

1. A Storm on the Horizon 15
2. A Near Miss and a Direct Hit 25
3. When Those Helping Others Needed Help 32
4. Homes in Its Path 41
5. Terror on Circle Drive 55
6. Heroes Came in All Sizes 76
7. A Building Stands Strong 90
8. A Strong Storm to the End 95
9. Extraordinary Survival Stories 102
10. Life-Changing Decisions 109
11. A Rescue of Immense Proportions 112
12. Recovering from a Disaster 122
13. Helping Becomes Second Nature 131
14. Those Who Were Lost 137
15. Three More Tornadoes 151
16. Other Stories 164

Index 185
About the Author 191

FOREWORD

Fifty years after the April 21, 1967 Belvidere Tornado, the memories of that day remain vivid in the minds of many. Some of their stories will be told in the pages that follow. Here's mine.

From our business on East Lincoln Avenue, I viewed the tornado sweeping across the south side of Belvidere, toward the high school. Knowing that my family would be out of harm's way, I jumped into my truck and headed toward the school to see if I could be of help. At the intersection of Logan and East Avenues, I could drive no farther. Downed power lines, trees and debris blocked the roadway. Proceeding on foot, I was soon asked to jump onto one of the fire trucks that was headed to the high school. We were among the first responders to the tragic scene.

Overturned school buses, damaged automobiles, parts of homes, trees and debris lay before us. I rushed to one of the buses to see if I could help. The cries for help and screams still resound in my mind. I lifted a small girl from the rubble and headed to the high school, where a staging area was being set up.

Four young high school boys miraculously carried a massive auto-hoist to one of the overturned buses to help raise it so aid could be given to those trapped inside. Classroom doors were being torn off the hinges so they could be used for stretchers to carry the injured.

Then the rain came again. The downpour sent people screaming and running to the damaged high school building for safety for fear of another tornado coming. The volunteers struggled in the mud and debris to continue the job at hand. The work continued until we were certain all had been found at the school. I was then asked to join a search group to check the damaged homes that were west of the school.

My clothes were wet, bloody and muddy. The cool air was chilling to my body. One by one, we searched the homes. One of the homes I searched was that of a local insurance man. I noticed his overcoat lying in the debris and quickly put it on, then continued searching. Darkness was starting to envelop the area. We decided to continue the search the next day. As I headed back to my truck, I was stopped by a local electrician and friend. He asked me to join him to go help some farmers who needed some electrical work done to get their power back so they could milk their cows.

It was nearly midnight when I arrived home. I was emotionally drained and physically exhausted. As I walked in the back door of our home, my emotions took total control over me, and I sat with my wife and sobbed.

The community came together that day and the days that followed. I had the overcoat cleaned and returned to the insurance man days later. He had not missed it.

Jerry Rowe
September 6, 2016

Jerry Rowe is a respected and admired Boone County native who had been reticent about sharing his experiences on April 21, 1967. The Belvidere Tornado Book Committee is grateful he has consented to share his thoughts in this foreword.

PREFACE

On a summer day in 2015, I dropped off all the archival material at the Boone County Historical Museum in Belvidere, Illinois, that I had gathered in 2007 while writing *The Belvidere Tornado: April 21, 1967*. While discussing the information with Anna Pivoras, the new museum director, and Lonna Bentley, a longtime museum registrar, they mentioned that the museum had none of the original 1,500 copies. Within a few moments, we all realized that the fiftieth anniversary of the most tragic incident in local history—one that still brings residents to tears so many years later—was coming up and that this provided an opportunity for a new book.

In the late summer of 2015, the board members of the Boone County Historical Society agreed to provide funding for this revised edition, much like they had done with the 2007 publication. During the process of writing proposals to publishers, the content of the book began to take shape. One of the initial decisions was to offer the perspective of time. Fifty years have passed since that horrible Friday in April, and our residents have seen three additional tornadoes in Boone County, occurring in 2008, 2010 and 2015. Therefore, it was decided the scope of the book should include those storms. And instead of a reprint of the 2007 publication, this book would include revisions of existing chapters, along with the inclusion of new information that was not available at the time of the original book.

In January 2016, the members of the Tornado Book Committee met for the first time, and a month later, the group began to seek stories, photos and other items relating to the four tornadoes that have struck Boone County. Through that process, several more sources were identified, and those additional stories have been added to this publication.

As with the first book, this book is the result of interviews, recollections, personal diaries, newspaper accounts and other sources available to the Tornado Book Committee members and the Boone County Historical Museum. It is an account of personal experiences from the tornadoes; it was not and never meant to be a complete historical document of the events of the tornadoes from 1967, 2008, 2010 and 2015.

ACKNOWLEDGEMENTS

Sources for the original Belvidere Tornado book included Joe Adam, Donna Bailey, Jane Ballok, John Bell, Ardella Beottcher, Betty Schrader Blake, Nancy Blankenship, LeRoy Blum, Joan Brannah, Fred Brereton, Phyllis Bresette, Brian Brockman, Rex Brockman, Carol and Edward Buhl, Larry Carlson, Teddy Carlton, Sheri Casey, Marty Chatham, John Church, Kathleen Boyd Clanin, Roy and Marge Coleman, Ken Conley, Ruth Craig, Shirley Craig, Sandra Cregeen, David Cummings, Sue Greenhow Dahlstrom, Bill Denning, Donna Denning, Ray DeWane, Joyce Drake, Norma Duclon, Kay Ellingson, Robert Ellison, Dave Englund, Debbie Ferin, John Fitch, Rick Frank, Lawana Wienk Fransen, John Gagliano, John Gallano, Louis (Ben) Giescke, Terri Glass, Rick Graham, Marilyn Grocen, Ed Grosvegnor, Alice Hajek, Barb Hammond, Donald Hanson, Sherry Page Hicks, Marge Hinrichs, Shirley Holley, Sue Holmes, Jeanette Huff, Aneita Ann Hurley, Virginia Hyland, Donna Hyser, Jean Hyser, Ken Johnson, Martin Johnson, Nancy Johnson, Florence Jordan, Jeanette Kastening, Teri Turner Keegan, Betty Kersting, Richard Knott, Jan Fiebranz Knutson, Judy Lamping, Jim Lantz, Nancy Lee, Linda Trueblood Lehman, Margo Johnson Licari, William Lindberg, Leslie Knott Lindsay, Gary Loofborrow, Stephanie Kokenes Loofborrow, Kathy Fitch Loy, Sue Lungstrom, Malvina Hart Lutz, Celestia Matheson, Ellen McHugh, Carol McQuinn, Joann Morse, Bob Nelson, Richard Nelson, Ken Nettleton, Dennis Norem, Ed O'Brien, Eleanor O'Donnell, Sonjia Luhman Olstad, Diane Onley, Maxine Osterberg, Arnold Pearse,

Becky Pearse, Shirley Pearse, Suanne Pfeifer, Bruce Poirier, Helen Poirier, Donald Pond, Bruce Poulter, Martin Powell, Marty Prather, Tom Pyszka, Dorothy Renn, Mike Robertson, Candy West Rogers, Ruth Knott Ross, Harold Ryman, Sherry Sandwich, Rick Schultz, Scott Schwebke, Connie Morris Shiroda, Penny Small, Mrs. Snyder, Ron and Karen Snyder, Judy Steinke, Steve Steinke, Cheryl Sturges, Judy Osberburg Sturges, Orin and Anita Thies, Roger Thompson, Jean Thornberry, Bonnie Nelson Thornton, Randall Trueblood, Gary Turner, Jim Turner, Alice Van Brocklin, Tim Wait, Joel Warner, Roxanne Wearmouth, Jack West, Jim West, Roger Wheeler, Russ Wheeler, David and Kathy Whitacre, Mary White, Terry White, Linda Wiggs, Pastor Eugene Wille, John Williams, John Winter, Peggy Wolf, Joyce Woody, Leslie Wright and Jerry Zepplin.

Sources for this book included Rick Anderson, DeAnna Bailey, Loretta Bates, Les Bellah, Shirley Carlson, Karen Cross, Pam (Wilson) Damm, John Darley, Peter DeWispelaere, Yvette DeWispelaere, Ivan Dye, Connie (Hernandez) Eloy, Donald Fisher, Ed Fritz, Beth (Dulgar) Funnsinn, Sandra (Mallett) Gray, Paul Greenland, Rhonda (Prell) Gunn, Barb Hall, Elizabeth Harris, Connie (Arnett) Johnson, Barbara Ann Kaiser, Adah Maurine Lindley Lepp, Pam Lindley, Renee (Prell) McClenthen, Roger Miller, Caitlin Nagel, Larry Nelson, Kimberly Radostits, Rocky Rouse, Jerry Rowe, Clem Schultz, Naomi Schultz, Diane Shattuck, Arlene Trimble and Rick Walraven.

The publications' accounts printed in the aftermath of the tornado used in both books include the *Belvidere Daily Republican*; the *Chicago American*; the *Chicago Sun-Times*; the *Chicago Tribune*; the *Gannetteer*; the *Milwaukee Journal*; the (Loves Park) *Monday Morning Mail*; the *Rockford Labor News*; the *Rockford Morning Star*; the *Rockford Register-Republic*; the *Rockford Register Star*; and "Storm Stories: The Belvidere Tornado" and "Windy City Tornado: Mega Disasters," Creative Differences Productions, Inc.

The past and present board members of the Boone County Historical Society who approved and supported the project are Marilyn Clanin, James Cox, Dr. Dale Drake, Robert Edwards, Micki Ernest, Dave Harbolt, Grant Michaud, Carol Rowe, Luis Salinas, Norma Schandelmeier, Naomi Schultz, Dick Stegmann, Ann Turner, Richard Van Evera, Judy Winter and Pam Zuromski.

This book would not have been possible without the effort of others, including Lonna Bentley, registrar of the Boone County Historical Museum; Roger Edwards of the Storm Prediction Center; Jill Fuller, former director of the Local History Room at Ida Public Library; local historian Martin

Johnson; and Sam Larson, sexton of the Belvidere Cemetery. Many thanks to the outstanding Tornado Book Committee members: Paul Arco, Lorna Collier, Sherry Hicks, Teri Keegan, Anna Pivoras, Drew Pivoras, Ann Turner and Troy Yunk. Lorna Collier, one of the best editors a writer could have, deserves special thanks for her dedication through the editing process. And finally, a great deal of gratitude to Anna Pivoras, who has worked with me on this project from the first day and through many meetings, e-mails and countless phone calls to bring to the readers the most compelling and factual information.

Chapter 1

A STORM ON THE HORIZON

Steve Steinke had a beautiful spring day to wash his car. So he spent the warm Friday afternoon hosing away the miles he had put on his 1967 Mustang during his forty-five-minute commute from Northern Illinois University to his hometown of Belvidere, Illinois. The twenty-year-old junior had just finished when he noticed the sky begin to darken. As an Earth science major who had taken meteorology classes, he knew that a change in weather could mean that his clean car was about to get doused. The change in conditions also triggered something else. "As a crazy weather guy, I had a habit of tuning on the radio to the lower AM band to see if I could hear any lightning strikes," Steve said. "The radio began crackling, so it was another clue that a storm was imminent."

It was April 21, 1967, and a storm was indeed brewing, but few were aware of its severity, its tragic path or the impact it would have fifty years later. Some, like Steve, who did have a clue of an impending storm, described small but noticeable changes. Diane (Anderson) Onley, an eighth grade student at Immanuel Lutheran School, recalled that the day was "humid and sticky, then it smelled funny." She had an inkling that something was wrong because it was so warm, saying, "In April, it's still cold out." Malvina (Hart) Lutz had been studying tornadoes and their effects in her eighth grade science class at Belvidere Junior High School. When she left school that day, she saw menacing storm clouds and decided to catch a ride home with a neighbor girl instead of taking

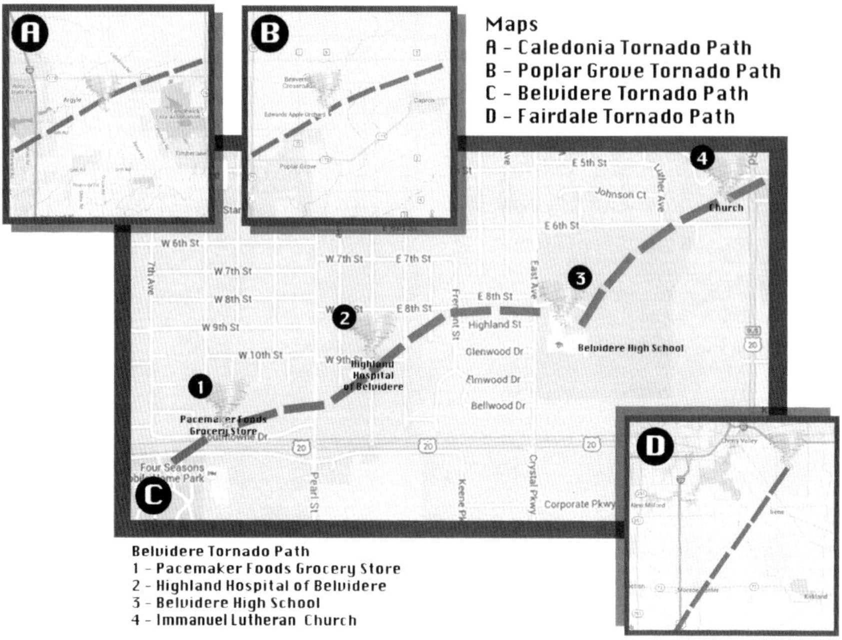

The paths taken by the four tornadoes that have touched down in Boone County. *Graphic by Troy Yunk.*

COMPARING THE FOUR TORNADOES THAT HAVE TOUCHED BOONE COUNTY

PLACE	DATE	FUJITA SCALE	LENGTH	MAXIMUM WIDTH	WIND SPEED	DEATHS	INJURIES
Belvidere	April 21, 1967	F4	28 miles	Half- mile	260 mph	24	500
Poplar Grove	January 7, 2008	EF3	13.2 miles	100 yards	165 mph	0	4
Caledonia	November 22, 2010	EF2	16.4 miles	200 yards	135 mph	0	0
Fairdale	April 9, 2015	EF4	30.3 miles	700 yards	200 mph	2	22

This chart compares the impact of each of the four tornadoes that have touched Boone County. The Fujita Scale (F0–F5) determined the impact of tornadoes until the National Weather Service devised a more impactful set of criteria in 2006, resulting in the Enhanced Fujita Scale (EF0–EF5). *Graphic by Troy Yunk.*

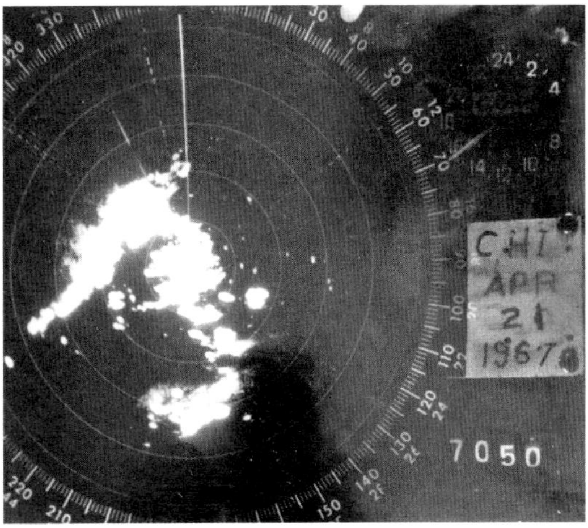

Storms of April 21, 1967, as seen on radar at a weather bureau station in Marseilles, Illinois, at the time of the Belvidere tornado. *Courtesy of Steve Steinke.*

the bus. But most in the northern Illinois community, with a population of about fourteen thousand, were unaware of what was coming.

In a span of roughly ten minutes, from approximately 3:49 p.m. to about 4:00 p.m., the killer tornado, designated F4 on the Fujita Scale, cut a ten-mile swath through manufacturing, commercial, residential and school areas of southeast Belvidere and Boone County. When it was over, twenty-four people had been killed, including seventeen children; more than five hundred were injured. More than one hundred homes and twelve businesses had been destroyed, with hundreds of others damaged. At least sixteen buses rolled over, many with children still inside, and became death traps. The cost of the damage was estimated to be at least $25 million, which is nearly $200 million today.

Steve is a trained storm spotter who first learned weather lore from his father, Larry. A thirty-year member of the National Weather Association, Steve served as the editor of the *American Weather Observer* from 1984 to 1997 and wrote weather reports and forecasts for the *Belvidere Daily Republican* for nearly twenty-five years. In April 1967, he lived on the 800 block of Fremont Street, about four blocks north of the tornado's eventual path but well within sight of the approaching storm. Even then, he knew what to look for. "Our home faced west, and I went out front to check out what I could about the movement of the storm," he said. "By watching the high cirrus clouds, I could see they would be coming in from the west-southwest. Within minutes, the sky turned an eerie green as the sun quickly and completely disappeared behind rapidly building cumulus clouds." Steve went back inside his home and told his mother that the storm was fast approaching, so they shut some windows. Then he took another look out the front window. What he saw through the budding but leafless trees was stunning. "I caught the rush of whiter clouds racing north on the low horizon. More clouds whirling around a wide dark core. I could not see all the way to the ground, but I knew this was a tornado. A wide tornado. And it appeared to be moving rapidly toward us."

Instantly, Steve knew he and his mother had to take shelter in the basement. But his mother insisted on calling his sister, Kay, who lived a few blocks away on East Avenue. The calls went unanswered. As the storm approached, the immediacy of taking shelter became paramount. Steve and his mother went to their basement, where they could hear debris hitting the house. Peering out of the window wells, he could see large pieces of debris flying through the air. "I knew the tornado was very close," he said. "The noises were unfamiliar. Breaking glass. Loud smashing sounds. And dull thuds, too." Then it became more intense. "The debris sounds were louder as larger and more pieces were crashing into our home. Peering upward through the window well, I could see the tall pine in our front yard just disappear. It had been there for decades. At the same time, our ears were popping, like those times when you are driving in mountains and, as you change grade, they fill and pop. We weren't going anywhere, and our ears were doing that. I knew that the storm was very, very close. And intense." Then it was over. Steve remembered some hail and rain squalls but no significant downpour. Conditions seemed to calm down. Through the basement window, Steve could see debris that had been carried high in the air "float more peacefully to the ground. I figured we had been spared the worst. The house was still above us. We waited another minute or two before going upstairs."

The Birth of a Tornado

The menacing cloud formations that Steve had seen from his front yard had also been seen by workers at Century Tool and Manufacturing Company at about 3:40 p.m. W.C. "Bill" Marander and John Jennings told the *Belvidere Daily Republican* they were on break at their factory near the corner of Route 5 (now U.S. 20) and Ipsen Road when they saw two massive cloud formations, one from the south and one from the north, collide in the southwest. When the two dark cloud banks met, the warm air from the south and the cold air from the north created a formation that began to rise in a circular motion. "Looks like a tornado," John recalled saying. Immediately, everyone there looked to the southwest and saw the formation seem to dissipate. Then, it formed again and the dark clouds merged into a blue-black cloud, then into a funnel directly south of the building. Bill said he saw a tail as debris began to spill out of the top of the funnel. Suddenly, Bill said, he felt a strong force, as the air from the southwest pulled him away from the building, but he was able to hold onto a door. At that moment, heavy rain and large hailstones began to fall. As the funnel started to move to the east, toward the Chrysler Assembly Plant, it grew larger and picked up speed. "There was tremendous counterclockwise swirling, rising movement," he said. "The funnel was not straight up and down. It seemed to lean in the direction it was moving." Awed, Bill watched as the tornado gained strength and moved toward Belvidere. As it moved out of sight, he had this thought: "I wonder if Belvidere was hit?"

It was. In fact, the tornado sucker-punched Belvidere, taking its first swing at the Chrysler Assembly Plant, where an estimated three hundred cars were damaged and siding was ripped from the building's exterior. It next struck the new Pacemaker Food Store. Assistant Manager Jack Stoll was rushing to his home in Cherry Valley when he was killed in his vehicle. He was the first fatality. The savage storm hit several homes before it laid waste to Highland Hospital, next on its incredible list of public buildings to be damaged. After plowing through several homes in a quiet neighborhood, it smacked into newly built Belvidere High School at the absolute worst time of the day, when students were leaving the new building and buses with elementary and junior high students were waiting to be loaded. At the high school, sixteen buses rolled over, some landing as far as one hundred yards away.

It then took a jab at another school, Immanuel Lutheran, destroying classrooms and ripping off the roof of the gymnasium. Several small businesses were also demolished near Logan Avenue and Genoa Road, including DeWane's Restaurant and Livestock Pavilion, which was filled with buyers at the weekly Friday afternoon auction. Then it continued its northeasterly route, crashing into farms before crossing Garden Prairie Road and into McHenry County.

Following their short wait, Steve Steinke and his mother went upstairs and got their first glimpse of the devastation around their home. Steve saw a two-by-four stuck in a neighbor's siding, awnings from his home hanging from their mount and the trail his tall tree left as it was dragged through neighbors' yards and over to Fourth Street, about seventy-five yards away. He saw a fire truck try to make its way up Caswell Street and the frustration

The darkened sky that produced a tornado is shown in this photo taken just prior to the tornado on South State Street. *Courtesy of Boone County Historical Museum.*

in the driver's face as he was unable to maneuver the truck past large debris and downed power lines. The driver was forced to turn the truck around.

It wasn't raining when Steve and his mother dashed toward Kay's house on the 900 block of East Avenue to check on her safety. On the way, he saw a painted piece of asphalt that had been torn from a roadway, papers, insulation, bricks, lumber, clothing, cardboard, shingles and many other random items. Steve and his mother found Kay was safe, her home intact. She had taken shelter in the basement. Steve hadn't realized at first that Belvidere High School, located a few blocks south of Kay's house at 1500 East Avenue, had been in the direct path of the tornado. But by the time he found Kay, he saw "clusters of confused kids…walking north and away from the high school area. Tears but not many words. Some were a mess with mud and dirt covering faces and arms. All were in shock."

Because of the extent of the destruction, streets were littered with debris, making passage for emergency vehicles difficult. "More emergency vehicles were now inching their way south between debris where they could," he said. "But there was no frantic movement of vehicles. No safe passage for anyone." Steve worried about the safety of his dad, a school bus driver, and his girlfriend, Kathy, who had been in class, and set off for the school to

This aerial photo shows the path of the Belvidere tornado through the neighborhood on its way to Belvidere High School. *Courtesy of Boone County Historical Museum.*

find them. By the time he got to Fifth Street, about two blocks north of the school, rain and hail began again. Steve took cover behind a pole from the hail and cold, driving rain. "The tornado had passed, but a trailing storm battered the area still," he said. "Misery was everywhere, and that rain was a cold rain. Now, driven by the damage I could see ahead of me, I kept moving south on the street." The hail stopped, and the wind eased a bit.

As he approached what had been the greenhouse in the 1000 block of East Avenue, he met up with his girlfriend, Kathy, and several of her friends. At first, he didn't know who she was. "I couldn't recognize her because of the mud and blood on her face, but she recognized me," he said. He comforted her, telling her the tornado was over, but that he had to find his dad's bus, Number 32, which usually picked up students on the south side of the high school each afternoon.

Steve was experiencing the chaos firsthand, the stunning nature of the first few moments following a disaster. He joined a tide of rescuers and worried family members inching their way to the high school, which had just opened its doors the previous fall. It was damaged but still standing. It was the site of the greatest loss of life that day.

"My mission to find my dad grew more intense when I crossed Sixth Street and saw the scope of the damage," Steve said. "Even worse, I saw school buses strewn around the open field to the east side of the road. Mangled. Upside down. On their sides. One even all the way out to the distant back fence…maybe four to five hundred feet from the school.

"I could smell natural gas and [saw]…a downed power line arcing into a puddle of water right on East Avenue. I thought, 'Why are they allowing these kids to walk right past that? Someone could get hurt.'" He only later realized the bitter irony of that thought.

Even with the pungent, potent smell of gas and the burning electrical wires around him, Steve's only thoughts were of his dad and whether he was all right. The closer he got to the school, the more he saw evidence of the tornado's deadly path. "I walked by a young boy, perhaps ten, who was sitting calmly in the grass of the open field," Steve said. "He had a piece of wood through his leg." Emergency medical workers were helping victims. "With others now tending to those who were bewildered and hurt, I walked right on by. Only long after the storm did I second-guess why I didn't stop to comfort him…get him help. I guess it was because he was sitting there so calmly, as though knowing help was on its way. And it was."

Steve then turned to the heartbreaking collection of battered, nearly destroyed buses on the northeast side of the school. He ran from bus to bus, looking for Number 32. "There were a lot of folks who were jumping in to help and tend to survivors, so I pushed on," he said. "I even walked all the way to the bus mangled up against the fence line on the far side of the field. Whew! It wasn't Number 32. *Lucky*, I thought…not even thinking about who might have been in it when it rolled and rolled to its resting place."

He rushed back toward the north side of the school, still frantically searching for his father, and saw something absurd: a handful of kids on the roof by the gym. He remembers thinking in his shock, terror and grief how foolish the students were being and wondered why they would be on the roof "on such a terrible day"—only realizing later that they had been blown up there by the tornado.

Steve decided to check the south side of the school where his father, Larry, picked up students. Rather than walk around the building, Steve took a shortcut through the hallways. As he passed by the gym, he saw another bus driver whom he knew. "I asked if he had seen my dad," Steve said. "He said that he had not. 'Not everyone made it,' he said. 'Those who didn't are in the gym.'" Hesitant but determined, Steve went into the gym to see if he could find his father. "Passing those covered but tiny bodies lined up on the floor was certainly unforgettable," he said.

Steve's walk took him past storm victims who had gathered in the halls and library of the school for safety and help. It was a devastating sight. "Kids of all ages were crying and sitting, mostly in silence, along the corridor and in the library," he said. "Mud-covered and wet, some were bleeding, but most were simply sitting and waiting. Other adults and kids were taking down hall doors to use as stretchers to lie across makeshift school bus ambulances out front.

"It was then that I finally realized the scope of the tragedy that had just unfolded. A new school destroyed. And in the dark of it all were bewildered and stunned people who never saw it coming."

When Steve got to the south side of the school, he was relieved to find out that bus Number 32 had never made it to the school that day. Larry Steinke had dropped off some students from Washington School and was turning onto Pearl Street from Locust when he saw the tornado to the south and made the decision to park right there. Seven-year-old Kathleen J. Boyd recalled what happened next. "When we turned the corner onto Pearl, Larry stopped the bus and told us all to get under the seats," she said. She looked up the street toward the Pacemaker and saw the tornado—"the most horrible thing. I can remember it as vivid today as I did that day. It is not something you easily forget."

It wasn't until midnight that Larry Steinke returned home to his relieved family. "He told us he had seen the tornado approaching," Steve said. "He kept his bus and kids safely away from the storm." Coincidentally, father and son had been at the high school at the same time—but hadn't seen each other. "He was asked to help identify the bodies in the dark, leaking gym," Steve said. "He accidentally brought home a wallet and ID of one of the child victims. He returned it to the police the next day."

While one family was safe, hundreds of others suffered death and injury. Of the twenty-four victims, seventeen were school-aged children. Thirteen of them were killed on April 21, 1967; four others died later. Today, it ranks as the sixth-worst school-related tornado disaster in United States history. The names of the children and all those who lost their lives are permanently recorded at a monument located outside Belvidere High School that was dedicated on the fortieth anniversary, April 21, 2007. Hardly a day goes by during tornado season when there isn't a new report of destruction from similar storms. However, Belvidere's tornado is a singular catastrophic event.

No one of a certain age in Belvidere and Boone County can ever forget where they were that Friday afternoon.

Three facts make this tornado one of the worst in our nation's history. First, it was part of a substantial front that day that caused storms in four states—Indiana, Missouri, Michigan and Illinois—and created at least seven tornadoes. In Illinois alone, twenty other communities were hit. There were individual deaths in Chicago and suburban Stone Park, but only Oak Lawn, with twenty-three killed, had nearly as many lives lost. A home in southeast Rockford was leveled as part of the storm cell. Second, Belvidere's tornado struck at vulnerable places at the worst possible times, hitting a grocery store, a hospital, two schools and several businesses, including a livestock auction house that was filled with people only on that day at that time. Incredibly, it smacked into Belvidere High School just as students were leaving for the day and buses were in line waiting to pick them up. Third, while there was a tornado watch issued, no official warning came until 4:03 p.m., well after the storm had swept its ugly path through Belvidere. It was a time well before cellphones and news immediacy.

Most of the public artifacts from that day can be seen at the Boone County Historical Museum. According to local legend, the car-sized dent that appears several feet above the ground on a metal grain bin on an Irene Road farm southwest of Belvidere is a reminder from that day. Aside from the tornado monument, few physical signs remain. What will never be forgotten are the stories of what happened on April 21, 1967—stories that are fresh today, fifty years later.

Chapter 2

A NEAR MISS AND A DIRECT HIT

Illinois is known as the Prairie State, and Boone County is part of the northernmost reach of the prairie. North of the Kishwaukee River, which angles across the southern part of the county, hills begin to rise toward the Wisconsin border, a mere twenty miles away. But south of the river and Interstate 90 and stretching for miles lie flatlands, which attracted the first settlers to this area in the 1830s. The Chrysler Assembly Plant was built on this prairie, adjacent to I-90 in southwestern Belvidere, and from his office window on the south side of the administration building, plant manager Jim Shepherd had a clear view to the southwest. Even today, the view from that vantage point is basically unobstructed, aside from a highway overpass, farm buildings, homes and silos.

Shepherd was on the phone on April 21, 1967, talking to the plant manager in Los Angeles, when, according to the *Belvidere Daily Republican*, he said, "You know, Otto, I think I see a tornado coming."

It was the first major storm of its kind in Boone County history but also the first of four tornadoes to touch down locally over the next fifty years. That, in itself, disputes a common local belief that the area is protected from storms that come from the southwest. These storm fronts typically are deflected north or south of Boone County because it lies in a geographic notch, between low hills to the southeast and larger ones to the northwest. However, since 1967, there have been three major tornadoes in the area of the notch: January 7, 2008, near Poplar Grove; November 22, 2010, near Caledonia; and April 9, 2015, near Fairdale. All caused damage, but

Above: The Chrysler Assembly Plant was the first major structure hit by the Belvidere tornado. *Courtesy of Boone County Historical Museum.*

Left: The distinctive half-round concrete roof sections of the Pacemaker Food Store that withstood the tornado are believed to have saved lives. *Courtesy of Sheri Casey.*

only one resulted in loss of lives. The Fairdale Tornado killed 2 residents in northern Ogle County, but the tornado's path extended into Boone County. Residents of Boone County are not alone in believing that areas are protected because of hills, rivers and the like, according to Roger Edwards of the Storm Prediction Center. "Many other towns used to have such myths before they were hit," he reported on his website, including extreme examples like Topeka, Kansas, which experienced an F5 tornado with 16 killed in 1966, and Waco, Texas, where an F5 killed 114 in 1953. Edwards could have included Belvidere. "Violent tornadoes have crossed rivers of all shapes and sizes," he wrote. "Tornadoes have crossed high elevations in the Appalachians, Rockies, and Sierra Nevada."

"We Knew It Was a Bad Storm"

At noon on Friday, April 21, 1967, the Chrysler Corporation completed its weeklong instruction for first-shift employees at the Belvidere assembly plant on what to do during a tornado. Little did anyone know that several hours later, a real tornado would bear down on the plant, which built its first car in 1965.

A few hours later, with menacing weather approaching, Jim Shepherd quickly ended the phone call, saying, "Oh, boy! I'm going to have problems." As soon as he put down the phone, his secretary popped her head into his office to tell him that she had just received a call about a fast-approaching storm.

"I know," he told her. "I can see it from here."

What Jim saw was a flat, broad storm formation with dark, heavy clouds. It seemed to be moving east, paralleling I-90 until it came even with the administration building. Then it turned and cut across the interstate highway. Jim continued to watch as the northern edge of the tornado reached the edge of Chrysler Drive, which runs in front of the plant—about sixty yards from his window. Jim said the outside edge of the tornado was a mass of hail and other objects, including sticks and limbs. It was very dark and about a quarter mile wide.

Inside the administration building, the rapid change in air pressure caused Jim's ears to pop. Doors swung wildly back and forth, another effect of the great change in pressure. The vents on the building's roof opened, allowing the pressure to equalize and, quite possibly, saving the roof and preventing glass from shattering. As the storm swept across the front of the administration building, Russ Wheeler, Rick Frank and the other second-shift workers were alerted by a tornado siren.

Russ, a second-shift supervisor in the final assembly area, knew what to do because of their training. "We all took cover in our designated areas," he said. "I remember that when we went to our [designated] safety places, the plant filled up with dust, and you could see parts moving on the racks." Rick rode out the storm in a stairwell.

"It was only about three minutes before it was over," Russ said. "We knew it was a bad storm. We didn't know the magnitude of it."

When it was over, Jim went into the plant to check for damage. There appeared to be no damage to the interior and no injuries in the plant. One man was injured at South Guard House No. 2, one of the small buildings that provided security to the sprawling plant. It was the only injury among the plant's 2,500 workers.

The Belvidere Tornado tossed this car into a ditch west of the Pacemaker Food Store. *Courtesy of Boone County Historical Museum.*

Once the all-clear sounded, workers attempted to continue their shift building new Plymouth Furys, Dodge Monacos and Chrysler New Yorkers. "They kept everybody in the plant for a while," Russ said. "We tried to start back up, but we had no power. When people started to leave, they couldn't find their cars."

Rick was stunned when he got to the parking lot and saw the destruction. "Cars were totally demolished where I usually parked my dad's car," he said. Eyewitnesses said they saw cars stacked two or three high.

The *Rockford Register-Republic* reported that damaged cars from the plant and those caught up in the storm while driving on I-90 could be seen in the nearby fields. "Autos lie rolled up in balls out in the middle of a farm field several hundred yards from their parking lot. Other autos are still strewn along the toll road and in ditches along cross roads," the report said.

Considering what could have happened, the Chrysler plant received relatively little damage, with most confined to its southeast corners. The upper section of the plant's southeast wall, which was the closest part of the building to the tornado, was blown away, and parts of the structural frame were exposed. Shepherd estimated the structural damage at $250,000 to $500,000. About two hundred brand-new cars also were

Workers cart debris out of the Pacemaker Food Store. *Courtesy of Sheri Casey.*

damaged, both in the lot and those already loaded on two-tier rail cars, six of which toppled over. About one hundred employee cars were damaged as well.

It could have been worse. At the time, Chrysler Corporation required its workers who lived in places vulnerable to tornadoes to attend weeklong training. Jim said the plant showed movies that dramatically depicted destruction by tornadoes, where to go and how to act. The instruction for the first shift ended four hours before the real thing happened.

And the timing was critical. By 3:50 p.m., the approximate time of the tornado's strike, all of the first-shift workers were gone and all of the second-shift workers were in the building. Had it hit forty minutes earlier, when workers were outside coming and going from work, "it would have been a disaster," Russ said.

"The Real Hero"

Anyone who has driven by Pacemaker Fine Foods store on U.S. Highway 20 in the last fifty years has noticed its distinctive roof, highlighted by half-circle formations. That unusual roof actually helped to save many lives the day of the tornado.

The Pacemaker grocery store was one of the first commercial ventures built in southeast Belvidere. Located on a service road off U.S. 20, it opened in 1964. On that Friday afternoon of April 21, about fifty workers and customers were in the store.

In the *Belvidere Daily Republican*, Ruth Kiefer, a checker, said she recalled customers coming in the store and describing the sky, thunder and lightning. "I could see the black cloud coming from the southwest through the big glass window," she said.

Carl Bangert, a store employee who had gone outside, saw the tornado approaching and ran inside to give a warning to twenty-five-year-old store manager Jerry Dal Pra, who got on the loudspeaker and told everyone a tornado was coming and to get in the corner where the bread rack was.

"The real hero of this thing was [Jerry] Dal Pra," said Carl.

"There were people everywhere," recalled Jerry. "They were all running. I saw one woman run toward the front door. I ran and tackled her and made her stay on the floor. Although there was a lot of confusion, everyone seemed to be fairly calm. I had to make the announcement only once.

"Some of the people flattened themselves against a wall at a big window. We got them up and into a protective corner. Then, all of a sudden, everything fell in. If the roof hadn't held up, we all would have been killed."

As workers and customers huddled in the corner, cement blocks began falling around them. "Woven wire was on top of us," Ruth said. "Some of us were holding up the wall. I have no idea how long it lasted." One woman became entangled in the blocks and wire. Then the floor gave way and a man and a woman fell through up to their chests. Ruth said the man was OK but that the woman's face was bloody. As people began to move away from the corner, Ruth noticed that many had blood and dirt on their faces.

"There were children and blood everywhere," said store owner Tony Dal Pra. "I saw the bread men with blood all over their faces, trying to dig people out from the debris."

The newspaper story gives this account of the rubble left by the storm: "Sections of uprooted walls were in jumbled stacks. In the parking lot, more than a dozen cars were demolished. Some contained bags of groceries abandoned by persons who fled back into the store."

Amid the screams and loud voices, there were calm voices urging people not to panic. Ruth noticed a friend sitting on a cement block. "I stopped to see how she was. She was in shock." Ruth found an opening in the east wall and climbed through the debris to escape. When she got to the parking lot, she saw that all the windows in her car were broken. "I knew there was no point in trying to get the car out," said Ruth, who then walked home.

According to historical records, one person, Sandra McClain, twenty-one, died as a result of injuries suffered at the store that day. The *Rockford Register-Republic* reported that Sandra died two days after the tornado from injuries sustained when a wall at the store collapsed. A store employee, assistant manager Jack Stoll, was killed as well after leaving the store.

Accounts vary as to why Jack left. One says that he was responding to a call for volunteer firemen in Cherry Valley, the other that his wife called him home because of the storm warnings. What is true is that his vehicle was blown off the road and he was catapulted out the front window. According to the news story, Jack was found about forty feet from his vehicle, with rubber casing from the front window wrapped around his legs. Because he drove right into the storm, he probably was the tornado's first casualty.

The storm destroyed the west wall of the store and heavily damaged the east wall. Tony Dal Pra estimated the damage at more than $200,000. None of the store's groceries were saved. "But we'll rebuild," Tony told the newspaper. "We'll have a bigger and better store."

The commercial complex also included another building directly east of the store, which housed a dry cleaner and other businesses. Inside, Michael Fadden and Harriet Pearson were credited with possibly saving several lives, according to the *Belvidere Daily Republican*.

Michael, the manager of Johnny-on-the-Spot Cleaners, spotted the tornado coming and pushed several customers into the store's boiler room area. "When I saw the funnel forming in the parking lot of Pacemaker, I froze for a few seconds," he said. Then he sprang into action. Harriet, a clerk, was unable to run for cover, so she directed four or five other customers to the floor and lay on top of them as the storm passed.

The tornado caused significant damage to the dry cleaner, but there were no serious injuries.

The buildings that housed the grocery store and dry cleaner featured an unusual roof, one that store owner Tony Dal Pra had read about and was interested in, said his daughter Sheri Casey. According to articles that appeared in the *Supermarket News* in January 1966, the roof of the main building was constructed of eighteen half-round sections of pre-stressed concrete, each 120 feet long and 10 feet wide. Inside the half-round sections were coated ground rock-wood insulation, which formed the interior ceiling.

"That roof that my dad had built held up and saved many lives," Sheri said.

Chapter 3

WHEN THOSE HELPING OTHERS NEEDED HELP

Licensed Practical Nurse (LPN) Eleanor O'Donnell began her shift at Highland Hospital at 3:00 p.m. that day. It had been dark and cloudy, but she recalled that the sun peeked out right before she started work, as she was receiving information about the patients she would be caring for that day.

"My assignments included the child in pediatrics, the lady next door and an admission for surgery coming in," she said. "I was an LPN. The inner court had two ladies in [rooms] 41 and 44, a gentleman in 47 and a lady in 53. The other rooms were booked for surgicals coming in later in the evening."

And so she began her shift. As she made her way to room 53, she turned to answer the phone ringing in pediatrics. While on the phone, she quickly glanced at the clock and saw it was 3:49 p.m. When she hung up, she saw that the lower part of the window at the end of the pediatric hall that faced west had blown open. Because it had been raining earlier, she went to shut it.

"As I closed the window, I looked out and saw what looked like dark smoke coming across the vacant lot from Pearl Street," Eleanor said. "As I looked closer, I saw our garbage shed, which was about the size of an outhouse and contained the hospital's trash cans, get picked up whole and thrown across the parking lot."

Eleanor watched incredulously as the shed across the street was picked up and became airborne. "I convinced myself that I was really seeing this, but it took me a second," she said. Once the realization came that she was

Highland Hospital was severely damaged in the Belvidere Tornado, including portions of the roof. *Courtesy of Boone County Historical Museum.*

The emergency entrance of Highland Hospital is occupied by rescue workers on the right and a National Guardsman on the left. Broken windows from the storm can be seen on both floors. *Courtesy of Boone County Historical Museum.*

An information desk at Highland Hospital is swamped with relatives and friends seeking information about the injured. *Courtesy of Boone County Historical Museum.*

watching a tornado, her nursing instincts kicked in. "I then turned and ran toward the nearest baby, who was in room 58," she said. "About the time I hit room 59's doorway, the wind hit, and I could not get the door to 58 open because of all the air pressure."

Jan (Fiebranz) Knutson, a medical secretary, said that Friday had been relatively quiet as everyone looked forward to the weekend. "Suddenly, our office manager, whose desk was located in front of a window facing Pacemaker, shouted that we should all get downstairs," Knutson said. "She noticed the threatening clouds forming and knew a bad storm was on the way. My first thought as I headed for the stairway was to call my parents and alert them."

But as she grabbed the door handle, the suction from the storm pulled the door from her hand, and it slammed shut. Jan never made it to the basement. As the head nurse ran down the hall, yelling, "Get down! Get down!" Jan dropped to the floor. "It seemed like an eternity. I thought we would all be dead. I wondered what it would be like," she said. "There was a roaring sound. All sorts of debris flew through the air. I was hit on the head by a picture falling from the wall."

At that time, Jan was wearing a blond wig, which was a fortunate choice. "After the storm, I found that the wig was embedded with glass," she said. "It had saved my scalp from serious lacerations."

The *Belvidere Daily Republican* reported that Highland Hospital office manager Ethel Miles said she glanced up at the window in her office, which faced west. "We saw the cloud form," Ethel said, "and then we had about eight seconds before the tornado hit. [Hospital superintendent Esther] Hawkey dashed one way, and the girls and I ran the other way." When the tornado hit, many staff members lay on top of patients to keep the debris off. "Everyone was quite calm," said Ethel, which she credited to the disaster training sessions they'd had.

The wind rolled Eleanor across the wall toward a desk, where she saw ceiling tiles, books, toys and other objects flying in the air. The wire-enforced windows on the doors of the ward didn't break, but the noise was deafening. "The noise was like the roar of a hundred trains," she said. "You thought your ears could not stand it, and then it was very silent."

When the tornado passed, she noticed debris all over, and her first thought was of the child in room 58—the room with the door that she had been unable to open due to air pressure during the early part of the storm. "I ran to the door of 58 and pushed the door open, and the child had slept through the whole thing," she said. "There was only dust and dirt in his crib. He was uninjured. I pulled the crib into the hallway away from any windows or doors and started up the hall."

Then she checked on the woman in room 53 and saw a horrible sight. "The elderly lady was covered with debris," Eleanor said. "Several large, barn-type beams, probably a couple of feet across, were lying on top of her and the empty bed." Eleanor rushed out of her room and continued quickly checking other patients. She found one elderly patient from room 47 who was outside his room, safe in the hall. "He said he didn't know if he ran out or was blown out." Still seeking help for the woman in room 53, Eleanor hurriedly checked other rooms, noticing such random things as a clock radio on a bed and a tall flower vase sitting on the sill of a window that had all of its glass missing. Calmly and coolly, a testament to her training, she continued to check on patients and fellow workers. When she went to the front of the hospital to check on two surgical patients, she ran into another nurse, Mabel Brooks, who appeared to be in shock. "She said, 'They're all dead. I saw the house fly away. Sharon's dead. They're all dead,'" Eleanor said. Another nurse caught up to them and said she was going to check on those injured.

Two other women escaped injury when large beams landed on their beds, said Eleanor. "Luckily," she said, "they were both in the lobby at the time, or they, too, would have been critically injured. Somebody was taking care of us that day."

She reached another wing, where she ran into two men, one a maintenance worker and another who worked in the lab, and told them that she needed help to move debris off the woman in room 53. Once that was accomplished, they moved the injured woman, who had a large wound, and her bed into the hallway. Again Eleanor encountered Mabel Brooks, still in shock. But Eleanor had no time right then to tend to Mabel. "We got a dressing on the lady's wound, and since everything was pretty secure, I ran over to the other wing and they said they were in good shape." So Eleanor assembled carts with dressings and other items to get ready to treat injured survivors.

Damaged but Functional

The driveway to the hospital was blocked with debris until volunteers, including one with an end-loader, came to clear a path to the front door. Eleanor continued to help the injured, who were eventually told to go to the basement, where doctors were doing triage. "We were down in the laundry, which had no power, no lights," she said. "The roof from the center wing, our surgical wing, flew off, hit our parking lot and went into our windows." Then, she said, medical professionals began to arrive to help, such as nurse Juanita Wolf, Dr. Smith, Dr. Dettmann and other day-shift nurses. "The men came in, and some of them crawled into the surgery area to pick up supplies for the injured patients and brought them back to the basement," Eleanor said.

"We pushed desks together in the records room and made a temporary minor surgery area," Ethel said. "It took about forty minutes to move all of the patients and supplies to the basement of the hospital."

The pharmacy was located in the basement, but it was locked, and there was a dire need for its contents. "A state cop came along, and I told him that I didn't have the key," Eleanor said. "He said, 'Lady, you want it open?' And he took his foot and kicked our door open. So then I had to stand and guard the pharmacy until somebody came."

Because the hospital had lost its power, there was concern about drugs that needed refrigeration. John Winter, a fireman from Winnebago, said that he and his crew helped set up a couple of tow trucks to run a generator to keep the drugs refrigerated.

After Eleanor was eventually relieved from duty, she ran into Superintendent Esther Hawkey, who grabbed her arm. Nearly in tears, Esther said, "Miller flew away." Miller was the night nurse, who had been sleeping in the far south end of the building. When the room was checked after the tornado, all that remained was a dresser—the walls and everything else were gone. Then Eleanor remembered seeing Miller go out to her car about 3:00 p.m. "Esther said, 'Why didn't you tell me?'" Eleanor said. "I told her I didn't know she was looking for her."

Miller arrived later and said she was in her car on Logan Avenue near the old A&P food store. She was forced to walk back due to the debris and damage in the streets. "[When] she arrived, she got a big hug because they all thought she was deceased," Eleanor said.

At first, the conditions at the hospital were dire. Though the hospital was damaged severely by the tornado, injured people still arrived, sometimes before the doctors. "We had forty-seven people brought in from the high school and forty-two adults," Ethel Miles said.

Jan Knutson shared the same memory, recalling that people, some covered with mud and blood, "flocked to the emergency room as soon as the storm abated."

Eleanor worked in the triage area, with nurse Nina Reeser and doctors Smith and Dettmann. "I remember a gentleman with a major eye injury," she said. "We had people come in whose cars rolled over on the way from Chrysler. Even though our building had major damage, people who lost their homes came in, and people who were looking for people came in. And it was a shelter for people who had no homes now."

Nina tried to make sure every patient was clean, but the conditions were far from normal. "I said, 'Nina, we only have a lead pencil trickle of water, and I don't know how long that is going to last,'" Eleanor said. "So we washed [only] what we had to suture."

Once the doctors came in, Eleanor said the hospital could help with suturing and other injuries but not with anything beyond emergency care. "We could suture and give meds, those kinds of things," she said.

It was approaching 5:00 p.m., and the emergency personnel were still treating injured persons in the basement, which had no power. In those days, the hospital also did not have emergency generators. Glenn Johnson, who was taking photos for the *Rockford Labor News*, provided help with his emergency light unit, which allowed medical staffers to work on those seriously injured. His photos of the procedures appeared in the April 28 edition of the weekly newspaper. "We had light from the outside, whatever came through the windows," Eleanor said. "But it's a basement…you know it's not really light."

She recalled a bus arriving from St. Anthony Hospital in Rockford carrying doctors and nurses. According to the *Belvidere Daily Republican*, twelve doctors arrived from Rockford and an additional five came from Freeport. Some stayed; some went to help at St. Joseph's, Belvidere's other hospital, which had not been damaged. The additional medical personnel allowed the Highland staff to treat more patients. Another dramatic photo in the April 28 edition of the *Rockford Labor News* shows five nurses rushing into Highland Hospital, all in white uniforms, one holding onto her cap against the wind.

Their House Blew Away

Two people with the most serious injuries—the man with the eye injury and the woman in room 53—were evacuated. Then, Eleanor was told to check on the rest of the patients waiting in the makeshift emergency room. One woman told Eleanor that her husband "blew away" at DeWane's on Logan Avenue.

Eleanor then met up with two little boys sitting on a cart. "They had no shirts, no shoes," she said. "The one was four or five years old, and the other was probably seven. [The oldest] had his arm around his little brother, and they were both shaking.

"I said, 'Are you hurt?' He said no but that their house blew away, and 'Our daddy said we had to stay here because he is looking for mommy and my sister.' I said, 'OK, you can stay. You will be safe [here].'"

Eleanor wrapped the children in a blanket and moved on, looking for others who needed help. "I went down the hall and was checking people," she said. "Most of the people down there weren't injured; they just needed shelter."

Once the State Street entrance was clear enough for emergency vehicles to arrive, the evacuation of injured people began, with the most critical first. At the same time, more doctors arrived to help. "We had lots of doctors," she said. "I can still see their faces. We started stabilizing and moving people."

"We started transferring patients to Rockford as soon as possible," Ethel said.

In the meantime, the kitchen staff came in with sandwiches and coffee they had made at home and dug out cookies that had survived the storm. "By shortly after 9:00 p.m., we had everybody out of the building, and they were feeding the rescue workers," Eleanor said.

Sometime later that day, the son of the woman in room 53 got to Highland, and Eleanor had to tell him his mother was injured and had been transported out.

"I have no idea how many people came in and were treated," Eleanor said.

"After they dug us out, the fire chief came in his little car and said, 'I guess we're not bringing you anybody,' but he did get transportation for the lady who was in labor and delivered several hours after she was transferred to St. Joe's."

The other baby story—the boy left alone in room 58—didn't have such a quick ending. The boy, born on April 5, 1967, had no identification when he was taken to Rockford Memorial Hospital. He was there for so long—three days—that the hospital issued him a new John Doe birth certificate. In the chaos after the tornado, his family was unable to find him. Then someone at Rockford Memorial heard about a Belvidere family, the Johnsons, looking for an infant boy who was in the nursery at the time of the storm. After contacting the Johnsons, the hospital told them to come over with the child's grandparents to do blood work to prove the child was theirs. Thad Johnson was then united with his parents and has the distinction of having two birth certificates.

At about 9:30 p.m., medical personnel were told they could leave. Unfortunately, such disasters can bring the worst out in some people. Workers were told that there were reports of looting inside the hospital. Eleanor said one nurse saw a boy running down the hall with a white clock radio. "She said, 'You put that down!' and he did and ran," Eleanor said.

After the hospital closed at 9:30 p.m., Eleanor said plans were to put guards in place to protect equipment and other things from looters.

A week after the tornado struck Belvidere, the Highland Hospital staff received a commendation from then governor Otto Kerner for its ability to continue to function throughout the disastrous day. "None of the inpatients at Highland Hospital were killed," Jan Knutson said. "All were transported to other hospitals or nursing homes."

Jan and Eleanor each had interesting things happen as a result of the tornado. Jan hadn't been able to reach her parents to tell them she was all right. So she asked a man to take a note to them. "He agreed, and my parents were notified that I was unharmed even before they knew a tornado had hit Belvidere," she said. "They had been at a grocery store on the north side of town."

When Eleanor got to her car to drive home, she realized that that day was Egg Day, which was every third Friday. Earlier in the day, the egg lady had delivered seven dozen eggs to her at the hospital, which she'd placed in her car. "I bought them for several friends," she said. "When I got the door open, there wasn't an omelet. I only had two cracked eggs."

Instead, in the capricious way of tornadoes, she found another calling card. "I had three bushels of debris from a home in my back seat."

Chapter 4

HOMES IN ITS PATH

Some people were home, some not when the tornado hit that warm late April Friday. Some were just passing through; some took refuge in the homes of strangers.

LeRoy Blum counts himself as fortunate for being at home. "As luck would have it," he said, "I was home from work."

LeRoy lived in the 1300 block of Warren Avenue, off Sixth Street and one block west of East Avenue, a short distance from the high school that had opened the previous fall. On Sunday, April 16, a torrential rainstorm caused water to leak into Blum's home, where he lived with his wife and five-month-old twin daughters, Julie and Jennette. So that Friday, he stayed home from work at Green Giant to clean up the water in the basement.

During the afternoon, as LeRoy hosed, swept and mopped the basement floor, the twin girls slept upstairs. Between 3:15 and 3:30 p.m., they woke up hungry. "We were so close to finishing our project that we decided to bring them downstairs," LeRoy says. "I let them sit with us in their little plastic chairs."

With the baby girls still in the basement, LeRoy and his wife went outside to retrieve some rugs that were airing out. As his wife started to walk around the south side of the garage, "she came running back and said there were two tornadoes heading in our direction," he said. "Of course, I didn't believe her and wanted to take a look, and she said that I had better believe her." So they both headed back to the basement, where their daughters were.

The power of the storm is shown in this photo of a school bus that has smashed into a home on East Avenue. *Courtesy of Boone County Historical Museum.*

An emergency vehicle makes its way through debris. *Courtesy of Boone County Historical Museum.*

The massive effort to restore basic services to a storm-ravaged community is indicated in this photo of service vehicles that poured into Belvidere, arriving in caravans from Chicago and other areas. Note that the trees have been stripped bare. *Courtesy of Boone County Historical Museum.*

As he looks back, Blum believes his daughters were in the basement because they were meant to survive. "I feel that was the only reason we really had those kids in the basement," he said, "because if we would have had to go to their bedroom, we would have never made it back."

LeRoy recalls his home being hit twice. The Blums were pressed against a wall under the front door. When they looked up, they could see the sky—the entire threshold and the front wall above them was gone. When he tried to get out of the basement, he found the stairs blocked with kitchen cabinets and doors. "I had to dig my way out of there," he said. And when he did, he looked across the street and saw that the house across from his that faced East Avenue was gone.

"The subfloor was remaining, but it had shifted on the foundation and the gas line feeding the house was ruptured," says LeRoy, who recalled that a man flagged down a fire engine and, somehow, got the gas leak plugged in seconds.

LeRoy continued to look around and saw an amazing sight. "I looked in the backyard and a saw a horse standing there," he said. "The poor thing. It didn't appear to be injured in any way, but it was stunned. It wouldn't move. It was like a statue."

The garage that his wife had started to walk around a few minutes earlier was gone, but his car was still there, right where he had parked it. However, all of its windows were gone, with all the glass on the inside.

LeRoy grabbed some blankets and went to get his wife and children from the basement. Before they got into the car, he grabbed some boards that he had found and placed them on the seats so they wouldn't be sitting on glass shards. He had to dig a trail out of his driveway to get to the road.

Though LeRoy had filled his car with gas that morning, he only got a short distance—to the corner of Whitney and Logan, by the former Methodist church—before the car sputtered and stopped. "I don't know where the gas went, but I did run out of gas there," he said.

LeRoy found an open gas station, filled the tank once again and drove his family to safety at his grandparents' home near downtown Belvidere. "They had heard a lot of sirens, but they didn't know what was happening," he said.

Later, LeRoy and his grandfather drove back to his home on Warren Avenue and made two trips to salvage blankets, clothes, baby formula and whatever they could. But not in LeRoy's car. "I never drove my car again," he says. Due to the storm damage, it was totaled.

With help from Rick Manley of Manley Motors, LeRoy said he was able to get more items out of his house until they were ordered to leave. Those trips back showed LeRoy how widespread the damage was.

Later he found out that his nephew, Lawrence Decker, seventeen, had been killed in the tornado.

"His older brother and sister were there, too," LeRoy said. "They did survive, but they had a lot of injuries—a lot of glass and punctures. It was very upsetting to hear that, of course."

But he knew that it could have been worse. "I just felt it was an act of God that we were saved," he said. "The chimney came down in the girls' bedroom. They would have been hurt if they would have been in there."

That Friday was Shirley (Turner) Craig's turn to pick up two of her three children and the neighbor's children at Washington School. She had planned to drive to the nearby Pacemaker Food store, but, she said, "I had my hair in curlers and didn't want to be seen. Plus, I was low on gas."

So she sat under the hair dryer in the kitchen while the kids—Tammy, seven; Mike, five and a half; and Carol, three years old—watched TV cartoons in the living room. Then, Tammy came in and said the picture on the TV was snowy.

"I told her it was just raining and that it would clear up," she said. "The next thing I heard was screams and glass breaking."

Shirley ran into the living room and found Tammy caught between the wall and the front door, which had blown open.

"I picked up Carol and had to pull Tammy out from the door....She was like frozen in shock. Having no more arms, I firmly told Mike to follow me, which he did, and we went to the basement until the noise stopped and things seemed quieter."

When Shirley came up from the basement of her home, she found a large tree limb in the front door and glass and grit all over the floor. Also, all the windows in the house were cracked and chipped.

"After a while, I went outside to check with the neighbors," she said. "There were wires and trees down all over."

Then she saw a neighbor boy, who told her about the devastation at the high school and that one of the bus drivers, Gilbert Julin, had been killed. Shirley realized that her niece Teri Turner rode his bus. "But the boy told me that there was no way I could get there to look for her with all of the downed wires," she said. "So I went back home and waited."

The Radio Brings Devastating News

In a nearby house, about a block from the high school, Mary Ann White was taking care of an older woman. Mary Ann was recently married and five months pregnant, and her husband, Terry, was in the U.S. Air Force in Turkey. Mary Ann was talking on the telephone when she started to hear things hitting the side of the house.

"I looked, and all of a sudden a brick came through the window, so I hung up," she said.

Mary Ann knew that she needed to get to the basement and knew that she could have made it—but she had another responsibility.

"I went back into this lady's room because she wasn't coherent enough to understand what was going on....I went back into her room to get her, and we didn't have time to get out."

Mary Ann and the woman she was caring for rode out the storm in the bedroom. "I just knew I wouldn't make it back with her to the basement because she didn't understand very much. So I shoved her under the bed, and I tried to crawl under as far as I could, being five months pregnant."

And then, she said, "everything came down on us. There wasn't much left of the house I was in. While I lay there waiting to be found, all I could hear were sirens and screaming and pandemonium in the whole neighborhood."

Mary Ann recalled that there wasn't much left of the house, but she did notice one thing as she was carried out. "They had a huge aquarium in the kitchen, and as we went by it, I noticed that all the water was gone, the fish were gone, the sand was gone and most of the house was gone, but none of the glass in the fish tank was broken," she said.

Mary Ann was taken to St. Joseph's Hospital, where a cut on her leg was treated. Then, she went into premature labor, likely due to the stress of the tornado, she said. Fortunately, doctors were able to stop the labor.

Mary Ann's chief concern was getting word to her husband, Terry, about what had happened. The family contacted the Red Cross right away, and Terry was hopeful of hearing news as well. He was half-listening to Armed Forces Radio in Turkey, and on the 9:00 p.m. news, he heard about a tornado that struck his hometown of Belvidere. Unsure of what he had heard, he

A poignant photo of a house that is open to all the world. *Courtesy of Boone County Historical Museum.*

Leaving little to salvage, this is an example of the damage done to a home by the Belvidere Tornado. *Courtesy of Boone County Historical Museum.*

stayed awake another hour to catch the 10:00 p.m. news. "They stated that a tornado hit Belvidere with a lot of loss of life, which concerned me," he said. "I didn't know what happened. I couldn't call. There was not a thing I could do but wonder if everyone was all right."

Terry went to the Red Cross representative on the base but never got any kind of information. Finally, U.S. congressman John B. Anderson, who represented Belvidere, was able to get a ham radio message to Terry. "They used a ham radio network to get the information across different stations, and I finally got the information two or three days after the tornado hit," he said.

Anderson became aware of Terry's situation. "Congressman Anderson came to the hospital and visited everybody," Mary Ann said. "He came and saw me, and I told him my dilemma. He is the one that finally got the word to Terry that I had been injured."

Terry wasn't able to return home until the next year. But when he did, he saw for the first time the son that his wife had safely delivered, a healthy baby boy named Kevin.

One of the most recognized signs in Belvidere at that time belonged to Realtor Betty Brenner. *Courtesy of Boone County Historical Museum.*

The ham radio network that helped Terry get the word about his family is another of those unrecognized groups from that terrible day. In an article in the *Belvidere Daily Republican*, it was estimated that ham radio operators in Belvidere passed about 175 messages with information about the health and welfare of local residents.

For local communications, four base stations were in constant contact with mobile units and the Red Cross, while at least three were handling more distant traffic. One ham operator had to build a new antenna because of damage to an antenna on his car; another helped to transport survivors to hospitals, despite not knowing about the condition of his own daughter; and a third used his radio to notify Commonwealth Edison that a power line was down and arcing. Before the utility located the downed line and shut power off, the ham operator stayed on site and prevented people from crossing the line.

Besides those in Belvidere, ham operators in Rockford, Milwaukee, Lake Geneva, Beloit and other nearby cities helped to bridge the communication gap by relaying or delivering messages.

No Birds Were Chirping

The bus dropped off Ron Ryman at the home of his grandmother Marjorie Ryman, who lived at 409 East Eighth Street, around noon. He was a kindergartner, and that day, there wasn't anybody around for him to play with. So he sat on the front porch while his grandmother baked a cake.

"It got so still," Marjorie wrote in a family history. "There wasn't a bird chirping or anything. I looked out the back window toward Highland Hospital [and the sky] was a greenish-black."

Marjorie called Ron to come in and got her cat, Miss Muffet, and "oh, yes, my purse, too." She gave Ron a flashlight, and they headed to the basement. Then the electricity went off and the basement was dark. "We went to the southwest corner of the basement, and we heard this awful noise," she said. "It hurt our ears. Then it sounded like a train had hit the house. Ron looked up at me and said, 'Ninnie, should we pray?' We did.

"Then we went upstairs, and I couldn't believe my eyes. The back door was gone, the garage was gone. All of the houses in the back of us [on Highland Street] were gone."

All the windows in the house, except for the picture window and the windows on each side of the basement, were gone, and the cake was all over the wall. The next day, family members were at the lumberyard at 7:30 a.m. to buy shingles and plywood for the roof.

"By 8:30 a.m., there were six men fixing our roof," she said.

Three days later, Marjorie had to have a tetanus shot because her limbs were embedded with tiny glass slivers. "It felt as if I had hundreds of slivers on my arms and legs," she said.

Incredibly, this was the third tornado she had lived through. "The first was in 1916 in North Dakota," she said. "The second in 1928 in East Rockford, and this one, April 21, 1967, in Belvidere."

Even today, drivers leaving Belvidere High School can avoid the traffic on East Avenue at the end of the school day by darting up one of the side streets—Highland Street or Glenwood or Elmwood Drives—so it wasn't unusual for Bill Denning, a junior at BHS, to follow that route.

"We went out of the parking lot north of the school," Denning says. "I had borrowed my dad's car, a 1954 Chrysler Imperial—a big car, lots of iron. I told Dennis Walters that I would give him a ride home.

"As we were leaving the lot, we looked to the west, toward the Chrysler plant, and it was very dark. There was a lot of traffic leaving school, so we said we're not doing East Avenue. We're going toward the Pacemaker."

The two teenagers drove west and then turned onto Glen Elms Drive. Bill, a busboy at the Huddle Restaurant, knew that one of the waitresses lived on Glen Elms. As they worked their way toward Pacemaker, they were driving directly into the tornado. "But we didn't know that," Bill said.

It started to rain hard, then large hail began to fall.

"They were like tennis balls, big enough that they were shattering the window of the car," Bill said. "I said, 'We've got to pull off the road,' so we pulled into a driveway on Glen Elms."

Bill realized that he and his friend had to get down onto the floorboards, but his friend was slow to react. "The wind kept getting stronger and it kept getting darker, and I'm yelling to Dennis, 'We've got to get down!'" he said.

As soon as they both dropped below the dashboard, there was a huge roar.

"The roof collapsed, but we were down enough so that we were OK," Bill said. "The windows were completely shattered. Both of us had gravel and stuff on our face and arms.

"The next thing I remember was that it was deathly quiet and that all I could hear was the natural gas hissing out of places where houses used to be."

When the two teens poked their heads out of the car, they were amazed at what they saw. The car still sat in the driveway of the house. But the house was gone.

"There weren't any houses anymore," Bill said. "Just the driveways. My dad's car was still there, and I credit that to the fact that it was a big hunk of iron."

When they got out of the car, they saw not only that it was totaled but also something even more unexpected. "There was a fork stuck into the side of it," Bill said.

Thankful She Ran Out of Gas

Mother of five Shirley Carlson had a carload of kids, with one more to pick up that day after school. "That afternoon, I picked up the kids at Washington School and went to the high school to pick up Debbie," Shirley said. She passed the junior high school on Pearl Street but didn't get much farther because her car ran out of gas. "I went to this house and asked if we could come in and call a taxi," she says. "About that time, it started to rain. I stood on the porch and saw a big black cloud coming our way."

Of course, the taxi never came, but Walter Fitch, driving by in a red pickup truck, told her they could all climb in. The group included her four children—Rhonda, Cindy, Mike and Valerie—and a neighbor's daughter, Terry Mason. Due to debris in the roadway, the truck could not get past Sixth Street. But they were a block away from home, so they walked.

"Terry's mom was glad to see us," said Shirley, who was equally glad to see her own oldest daughter was at home once they arrived there. "Debbie was home, sitting by a large picture window," she said. Debbie's dad, Ron Carlson, had called and told her to go to the basement because a tornado was coming. "Then the phone went dead," said Shirley. Debbie had taken her father's advice and stayed safe. Aside from two large windows that were shattered, their home was undamaged. The next day, they drove back to Pearl Street and found their station wagon badly damaged by hail.

Looking back, Shirley knows how fortunate they were. Their daughter Debbie survived at home alone. But a younger daughter, Rhonda, lost one of her classmates, Cristine Lutzow. That Sunday, Shirley said, "we all went to church to pray for everybody, the victims, and to thank God that we were all OK." And to this day, she thinks about what would have happened had she not run out of gas. "God was looking over us," she said.

Ed Fritz had just finished his day at Belvidere High School and was unloading a batch of towels with a friend, Greg Popp, for an upcoming car wash. Greg lived across from the high school on East Avenue, and as they unloaded Ed's car, another car pulled up to the curb and two students yelled and pointed in the direction of Highland Hospital. "We looked up, and there were three large funnels over the hospital, which was being heavily damaged," Ed said. "Greg and I ran into his house, where his little brother was watching TV, totally unaware of what was coming. While Greg ran through the house, opening windows like we had been taught in school drills, I grabbed his brother and ran down the stairs to the basement. We rolled under a table against a wall and held on. Greg came jumping down the stairs and rolled up to the wall just as the tornado hit. It was a short chaotic sound, like the often-described freight train, coupled with the squeaking sound of hundreds of nails being pulled out. The concrete basement wall I was up against lifted and then came down."

A few minutes later, they climbed the stairs to find only walls of the bathroom standing. Everything was gone. "The furniture, appliances, walls and even the flooring down to the subfloor was gone," he said. "They weren't just lying in the yard; they were gone."

As Ed walked toward the high school to see if he could help, he saw some unforgettable things:

- One of his classmates "literally rose up out of the mud" in the ditch he had gone to for protection.
- A car had a two-by-four driven through the windshield and buried into the back of the driver's seat. Fortunately, the car was empty.
- A horse ran by with a chunk of wood embedded in its flank.

Ed made his way to the gym, where he comforted the many injured. He applied an ice pack to the head of a young boy, injured on a bus, until help arrived. "I continued to help move victims and do what I could with them," he said. One girl was screaming, trying to get out of a doorway, but a metal bar held her back. "We helped her back to the gym," he said. "Eventually, I left the area to meet with other students and try to understand what had happened." The next day, he found his and Greg's cars were "beat up but drivable," he said. "Eventually, Greg spray-painted 'Johnny King Thrill Show' on the side of his car, after the car show popular at fairs."

"Mom, what's that?" The question came from Deanna Bailey's daughter Shelli, who was looking out the front window of their home on West Tenth Street behind the Pacemaker Food Store. Deanna recalled, "I looked out calmly and said, 'It looks like a tornado, sweetheart. Get down.'"

They dropped down and hunkered in below the picture window as the tornado hit. When they stood up, they were amazed by what they saw out the window. "All of our neighbors' houses were practically destroyed," she said. "Ours was the only one intact, and we hadn't even had time to get into the basement! Furthermore, we took refuge right below a window." Deanna and Shelli had been packing for an overnight trip to her parents' home in Poplar Grove while Deanna's husband was on a camping trip. Their home sustained about $4,000 in damages. "The following weeks were rather lonely, as we were the only ones in our neighborhood who could live in our home," she said. "It was a long time before we had neighbors again."

An Open Door Saves Lives

Judy (Gorham) Lamping left school right away that day—before the tornado struck. A neighbor, Shirley Ferguson, had seen the threatening skies and decided to pick up her daughter and other neighborhood kids from Maple Avenue. In the car were Sally (Ferguson) Pavlak, Cheryl (Ferguson) Grayson, Linda (Ohlsen) Lyford, Judy, Judy's brother Jim and Shirley. All the kids were high schoolers.

They were about two blocks west of school when they started to see objects flying in the sky. Shirley said, "Oh my God!" and pulled the car full of teenagers into the nearest driveway, not knowing whose house it was.

"She made a quick right turn and saw a garage door open with no vehicle in it," Judy said. "She pulled the car right in and told us to get out. It was an attached garage. She turned the door knob to the house and it opened. All of us kids tried to follow."

They saw the basement door to the right, which Shirley opened, and Jim followed and held the door from the inside. But "as Jim held the door open, it was quickly sucked shut," Judy said. "He said they tried to push it open but couldn't budge it."

That's when the tornado hit.

"Sally and I were thrown on the floor of the small entryway as Cheryl and Linda laid on the stoop of the doorway," Judy said. "It came as fast as it went."

In the basement, Jim and Shirley heard a terrific roar. "It was us girls, screaming," Judy said. "Shirley said that all she could think of was at least we were screaming and still alive."

When Jim and Shirley opened the basement door, they were amazed to see the girls and the doorjamb of the basement—but nothing else. "The walls were gone," Judy said. "It was as if we were standing outside.

"One of the girls started screaming as she saw the buses all over the school grounds. She had a boyfriend, now her husband, on a bus. Shirley slapped her and told we had to get out of there."

Before they left, they noticed a bird in a cage unharmed and watched as a dog ran up to them. "So Shirley put the bird and the dog in the basement and shut the door," Judy said.

The car was demolished and the garage gone, so the group started to walk home.

"We were all scared, not fully understanding what had happened," she said. "Cheryl kept crying as somewhere her shoes had been torn off, and her feet were bleeding from walking on all the glass. I remember seeing people everywhere, walking and crying, coming from homes that were now gone. Shirley kept pushing us along, saying, 'Keep going. Watch out for downed wires.'"

The group of survivors crossed South State Street, then Pearl. When they turned the corner onto Maple, all the neighbors standing outside saw them and shouted, "There they are!"

The teens reunited with their families, and all survived "because of Shirley," Judy said. "A few cuts, bruises and tetanus shots were all that was needed."

But the story doesn't end there.

When Ken and Shirley Ferguson returned to the shattered home to get their car and belongings, they ran into the homeowners. "They said someone was definitely watching over all of us that day," Judy said. "They stated that they never left their home without locking up. Let alone [that] the garage door was left up."

The homeowner had no explanation for how or why the Fergusons found their home unlocked, with the garage door open, just as a tornado roared overhead.

Chapter 5

TERROR ON CIRCLE DRIVE

Malvina (Hart) Lutz, who had been studying tornadoes and their effects in her eighth grade science class, decided not to ride the bus home that day because it looked like it was going to storm. Instead, she got a ride with a neighbor girl. Once she got in the car, she found that the girl's mother had to stop at the high school to pick up an older sister. "That sounded OK," Malvina said. "I had never been to the high school. It probably wouldn't take that long, and I'd be home, safe and dry soon."

They piled into the station wagon, books, notebooks and purses on their laps, and drove to the new $3.5 million high school. The school, opened only months earlier, was the pride of the local community.

The creamy yellow brick school was built on the southeast edge of the growing community of Belvidere. Located on East Avenue, just north of Route 5 (now U.S. 20), it was fronted by a huge U-shaped driveway system. Everyone called it Circle Drive.

In the afternoon, buses, many containing elementary and junior high school students, picked up high school students at three places: Circle Drive; south of the school in the faculty parking lot; and north in the student lot by the gym. There were students not only from Belvidere schools in the bus but also two private schools, Immanuel Lutheran and St. James Catholic.

Circle Drive was also where parents and others parked to drop off or pick up students. It was actually a half-circle, and at the top was the main entrance to the school, a hallway that connected the classroom portion of the building to the gym.

One of the sixteen buses that was rolled over by the tornado. This one has been ripped from its frame and had its roof flattened. *Courtesy of Boone County Historical Museum.*

Shoe gone and sock wet and muddy, this little girl gets a lift to safety. Many students lost shoes that day and never found them. *Courtesy of Boone County Historical Museum.*

Students, parents, survivors and others leave Belvidere High School, which may have lost letters in its name but survived structurally sound. *Courtesy of Boone County Historical Museum.*

As they sat in the car in the rain and waited for her friend's sister, Malvina recalled chatting about the tornado facts they had learned earlier in the day. "It seemed impossible that our teacher had said [what] a tornado would do with its wind speeds," she said. "I remember we even laughed about it."

Although the rain let up, the sky began to turn "funny-looking, greenish" colors, and when the girls turned around in their seats, Malvina recalled saying, "Do you see what I see?" What they saw was a "many-funneled tornado heading our way! It was black with at least three tails and, at that time, was probably between Pacemaker and Highland Hospital."

They looked into each other's eyes and at the scene outside. "Run toward the school!" shouted Malvina's friend's mother. The girls did, leaving their books, notebooks and purses.

At about this time, many recalled hearing police sirens coming south toward the high school on East Avenue. They came from Belvidere police captain Francis "Dutch" Whalen, who was in a police cruiser a block away from the school when he spotted the tornado to the southwest. He was responding to a radio report from Officer Harry Faris, who saw the tornado hit the Chrysler plant from his vantage point at the Pacemaker food store. In the *Rockford Register Republic*, Whalen said, "I turned on the red light and siren and started yelling at the kids to get back into the school building. More than a hundred of them stampeded back into the school. When it hit, I was in the squad car praying. It took out the windshield, and I saw what looked like a house go by. Cars with kids in them were scattered all over."

The distance from the car to the school wasn't far, but Malvina recalled that time and fear made it seem like they were moving in slow motion. "People were running and screaming," she said.

Just then, confusion! Malvina said the school's fire alarm system went off, and students streamed screaming from the building. Joel Warner, a BHS freshman who was in the office serving an after-school detention, remembered that someone pulled the fire alarm. She also reported that the alarm had been pulled, probably by someone who thought he or she was doing the right thing. The result was what Malvina saw: many students running out of the building when they should have been inside, protected from the vicious storm. "It was a costly lesson," said an unidentified school official.

But Malvina never changed direction—never turned her head. "I never looked back at the car or approaching tornado," she said. "I don't remember hearing a roar or a train sound. I heard screaming and a fire alarm. The closer I got to the entrance, the harder it was to move, like the suction of a vacuum cleaner was after us. I had the sensation of lifting up a little. I grabbed hands with another child running on my left side. We made it into the high school building."

In the Middle of the Eye

Don Pond and Alice Hajek heard Dutch Whalen's warning, too. Pond was driving on East Avenue with some friends when, he recalls, "Dutch Whalen was screaming for everyone to take shelter."

Don, Randy Elliott and Ken Bowley turned back toward the high school, and en route, they met Gary Morris, who was walking. Just before the tornado hit, they pulled into a driveway—and the car slammed into the garage door.

"We couldn't stop the car," Don said.

Students evacuate the high school, making their way to safety along Circle Drive. *Courtesy of Boone County Historical Museum.*

When the tornado hit, it knocked out all of the car's windows, and the four boys were blasted with debris. During what Don called "the eye of the storm," when the wind died and it seemed to be over, they stood on the trunk of the car, but then they hurried back into the car when the second part of the storm hit them.

If the boys had felt bad about knocking down the garage door, it really didn't matter afterward. "The house was gone," Don said, "and the garage was gone, too."

Above: This picture, taken from the roof of the high school looking west, shows the damaged neighborhood that has been swept away to give a clear view of Highland Hospital in the upper left. *Courtesy of Boone County Historical Museum.*

Left: An adult helps young storm survivors after the storm. *Courtesy of Boone County Historical Museum.*

Alice Hajek was in front of the school in her Nash convertible, waiting to pick up her two daughters, Donna and Linda, and a neighbor girl. Alice's car was parked across the street from the high school, facing south.

"We were sitting there when a policeman came down the road," Alice said. "He rolled up beside me and told me to take cover and said that there was a tornado coming."

By this time, Linda and the neighbor girl were in the car with her. Alice looked around, considered going to the nearby house and then decided to make a run for the school. The neighbor girl stayed in the car, while Linda and Alice dashed toward the high school.

"We started running toward the high school, toward the gym," Alice said. They ran across a grassy area that had just been seeded, getting Alice's canvas shoes muddy. She told her daughter to go on ahead, that she'd be right there. But Linda stuck with her mom nonetheless.

Before Alice had left the car, she had glanced to the west and saw the tornado bearing down on the Pacemaker store and then decided to head for a door leading to a gym hallway. But when Alice and Linda reached what they thought would be safety with the tornado nearly on them, they found the door was locked. "There was no outside handle," she says. The doorframe, however, did have a window.

"So we pounded on the door, and a friend of our son's came running down the hall, saw us and opened the door," she said.

When they got inside, Alice and Linda lay down in a doorway of the gym hallway just as the tornado struck. "There were six of us, and we lay foot to foot, back to back, on top of each other," Alice said. "The neighbor boy was on the bottom, and I was on the top. We laid there and listened to the roar and the cracking glass."

When it was over, Alice looked down the hall to the door they had come through. "A car had been blown up against it," she said. "It probably would have smashed us into the building."

As survivors began pulling wrestling mats into the gym for the injured, Alice helped out, too. She wanted to start looking for her other daughter, Donna, but a gym teacher, Mrs. Lorene Benzel, had a job for her.

"Mrs. Benzel was wonderful. I started to look for Donna, but she said, 'No, you come here in the gym and stay by this girl,'" Alice said. The girl had broken her shoulder on her bus. "I stayed with her, and she cried and cried. As long as I talked to her, she was quiet. But the minute I stopped, she cried.

"By this time, they were taking the doors from the rooms and using them as stretchers. I stayed there until things sort of quieted down."

Alice and Linda left the gym and headed toward the library, which is where they found Donna, who had lingered in the building after school to talk to secretary Lorraine Martin.

"It was my parents' wedding anniversary, and they had plans to go out with Lorraine and her husband," Donna recalled.

While Donna, a junior, was there, Lorraine noted the threatening weather and suggested that she wait until the rain stopped. "Me being the typical teen, I just thought, 'Well, I'll get wet,' so I didn't pay any attention," Donna said.

But she did pay attention to the reaction of students and teachers after she left the office and walked down the hall toward her locker. "I noticed that in every room I passed, teachers and students were running to the windows," Donna said. "When I got to the last room, I saw that a teacher was there, so I went in and looked out the window.

"While I was looking at the sky, I saw four huge funnels drop out of the sky—one, two, three, four. They were the kind of funnels that were huge across the top, then came down to a narrow point."

Donna and the teacher quickly went toward the library, where they were told to find other shelter due to the glass there. She ran to her locker.

"When we got there, they told us to get out of the main hallway and get up against a wall," she said. "I was with my friend, who was a good trumpet player, and I held her trumpet. My friend Chris said to let go of the trumpet, but I couldn't. I think my brain was saying that the trumpet was normal, and that was the only reality I knew just then. So I held onto the trumpet."

Donna remembers the horrible roar of a train, an incessantly loud sound and then the sound of things bending and creaking and glass shattering. "We stayed until it was quiet. It was deathly quiet, morgue-like," she said. "The contrast is very real for me. I knew my mom should have been outside. My brain said to go where my mother would be waiting."

Still holding onto the trumpet, she and her friends went to the library to see if they could help.

"Nobody knew what to do," she said. "It was a horrible feeling of helplessness."

She saw survivors, some limping, covered with mud, tar and blood, carrying one another. "We tried to help those kids walking in," Donna said. "We laid them down in the library. After a few minutes or maybe a half an hour, it seemed like I should start trying to figure out how to get home. When I walked out of the library, I saw my mom and sister instantly."

As for the car, Alice's husband looked for it later. He found it about two and a half blocks from where Alice and Linda had left it. "It went down the street and around the corner," Alice said. The car then landed on the front steps of a nearby house.

And as for the neighbor girl?

"She was in the car the whole time," Alice said. "She rode it out, then got out of the car and walked home through all of the debris. She wasn't hurt."

Incredible Explosions...Then Quiet

Friday was band day, so Sherry (Page) Hicks, then fifteen, had her clarinet with her. She and Melinda Carlson were going to catch a ride with Melinda's mother. "We were sitting in the car, waiting to pull out from the Circle Drive," she said. "It was windy, hot and humid that day, balmy and stormy. We looked [west] through the subdivision and over the hospital and saw mass quantities of dark clouds rolling in, and I recommended that we all get out of the car and go back into the high school."

By then, the simple task of retracing their steps back to the main entrance had changed dramatically. "For every step we took, we were dragged back," Sherry said. "It seemed like it took forever, that we were never going to get back inside the building. My girlfriend was about eighty pounds wringing wet, and she held onto the back of me. Her feet, I swear, went straight out behind her."

Finally, they were able to get into the school and to the shelter of the nearby locker bays. "Then, someone grabbed us and literally threw us down to the ground and got down on top of us," she said. "We had no more hit the ground when we heard the biggest explosion you ever heard in your life. Every window in the place blew out. It was moments of explosions and glass breaking and screaming and crying...just an indescribable few moments."

That was followed by quiet. "Then, everybody stood up, and you didn't know what to do," Sherry said. "You were flabbergasted as to what just happened. It was just a moment that you didn't know how to recover from. It was bad. It was really bad!"

Sherry and others went to the nearby library, located at the time on the first floor, and sat down. Adults worked to calm the students and came through looking for people with injuries, who were taken elsewhere in the school for treatment.

Like others, Sherry was tattooed with tar and glass, her clothing torn off. "I had a three-piece corduroy suit on that day, but my skirt was missing, my shoes were missing," she says. "I had a slip on. The jacket from my suit was missing. God knows where that went. Instruments and everything else we left in the car."

To this day, Sherry doesn't know what made her get out of the car. "My girlfriend's mom said, 'Oh, we'll be all right.' I said, 'No, I don't think so.'"

Sherry was right. The car they were sitting in was carried away toward the athletic field, its top smashed. "We definitely would have been very injured or possibly killed if we would have stayed there," she said. "I just had a feeling that this didn't look good."

"I Hollered, 'TORNADO!'"

Among many people waiting in cars on Circle Drive that afternoon was Belvidere fire chief Jim Lantz, who was picking up his daughter Dana. He was doing what most of us do in that situation, sitting and listening to the radio, when he heard Whalen's police siren coming up East Avenue. Thinking that a student needed immediate medical attention, he got out of his car. What he saw stunned him. "I saw the tornado coming from the west," he said. "I saw three funnel clouds coming across. I hollered, 'TORNADO! We've got to get inside and get shelter.'"

As he got about halfway up the drive toward the school, he saw a woman in a car. "She said, 'What will we do?' I said we had to get into the school," Jim said. "I wanted to help the woman, but she wouldn't let go of the car door handle. She said her aunt was in the car and that she didn't want to leave her. I grabbed her hand, but she wouldn't let go of the car. So I finally took off because she wouldn't move."

The delay put Jim directly in the tornado's path, catching him about halfway between the drive and the building. "I took quite a ride," he said. "It picked me up, then threw me down, and then picked me up again."

He said that during his "ride," he recalled seeing debris flying around him. When he was dropped to the ground the second time, he thought it was over. "I was lying down in the grass, and then I raised my head and saw that I was lying right in the middle of it," he says. "All kinds of stuff was going around me in a big circle."

Incredibly, Jim realized he was in the middle of the vortex and that he needed to find something to hold onto.

"I looked over and saw a Ford; I don't remember what model it was," he said. "I saw the exhaust pipe coming from the bumper, so I grabbed the bumper and held onto it so I wouldn't get hurt so badly with the things that were hitting me."

But Jim went for his third "ride."

"It took the car and took me up again," he said. The last tumble knocked him out, and he was awakened by the rain. "I got up, staggered toward the school and realized that my shoes were gone," he said. "I looked down, and my necktie was gone, but my shirt was still buttoned to the top."

Dazed, he still made his way into the school and found his daughter and her friend, neither of whom was hurt. By that time, emergency personnel were arriving, and some of Jim's firefighters saw his condition and took him to Highland Hospital. "When we got there, we found out that it had been hit, so I said just take me home," Jim said. "I'll take a shower and find out how badly I'm hurt. When I got home, I found out my wife and the neighbor lady had been looking for me."

The two women cut Jim's shirt off because he couldn't raise his arms; both collarbones were bruised. His arms had many cuts and bruises from debris, but his shirt wasn't torn. "It drove stuff right through my long-sleeved uniform shirt," he said. "All of my back and shoulders were cut up. The next day, there was a mass of scabs on my arms, but it didn't tear the shirt." That night, his family took Jim to St. Joseph's Hospital to be checked over and for treatment of his minor wounds, but despite three rides in a tornado's vortex, he wasn't seriously hurt.

A Day When Seconds Counted

Timing was everything that day. A few seconds here or there made a difference in whether some people lived or died. Jim Lantz lost critical seconds as he tried to help a woman who wouldn't leave a car, and he was caught by the swirling, deadly winds. Malvina (Hart) Lutz didn't delay a second in her effort to get to the front door. Sherry Hicks said that others realized seconds counted as she made her way into the school. "I'm sure there were other people initiating the fear, even more so than you saw, that you had to get back inside to take cover," Sherry said.

But even that didn't ensure safety because, at some point, the wind pressure was too great for those holding the doors open. "There were people in the hall, men, making sure that people got back into the building," Sherry said. "The doors were open for you. You just had to get there. That was the challenge."

Jim Barr, a driver education teacher, was one of those standing at the front door of Belvidere High School that day at 3:40 p.m. In an interview with the *Rockford Morning Star*, he said, "We could see something coming, not knowing it was a tornado. I ran to the front door and opened it up. There were a bunch of students out front getting ready to load onto the buses. I yelled, 'You've got to get in here!'"

Jim said he held the doors open as long as he could until the glass in the doors started to break.

"I let the door go and dropped to my knees. But I know that some kids were unable to make it in there. That bothered me for a long time. I remember a boy trying to get in. But the wind was so strong that it picked him up—almost gently—and put him against the brick wall." Jim said that he never found out what happened to the boy.

Martin Johnson told a similar story. Martin, who was in Arty LaBuy's mother's 1964 Chevrolet in the north parking lot, recalled that his brother William also helped to hold the doors against the wind. "[A boy], who was outside behind him, was not strong enough to pull the doors open," Johnson said. "After the tornado, he was found dead upright against the door."

"We Thought She Was Dead"

Linda (Trueblood) Lehman was on Circle Drive, too. Like Lutz and Wright, she was in a car with friends, including Bonnie (Nelson) Thornton, but she can't tell the story firsthand like they did. Her memory of that day, and several days afterward, was constructed from stories told to her by others. That's because Linda suffered brain damage after she was flung out of an airborne car, flung into the tornado itself and tossed into the mud.

Bonnie recalled that all of the air was sucked out of the car when it was picked up by the tornado. Three of the girls were sitting in the back seat, and when the car landed, Bonnie said that one of the girls was unconscious and "the other girl [Linda] was in the mud.

"The storm drove her into the ground. We thought she was dead."

Martin Johnson and some friends were wasting time on that Friday afternoon after school listening to music in LaBuy's car. They were in the parking lot behind the gym, one of the three bus staging places. Some students, generally those heading to their homes south of the high school, were picked up at the south end, while those who lived in the northern part of the district loaded at the north side outside the gym. Other students boarded buses on Circle Drive.

The high school was the last stop on the city route, and buses had arrived already loaded with younger children from the public and private elementary schools and the junior high. This was the first year the high school had been open, so the parking lots were freshly paved, the roofs recently completed and the grass freshly seeded.

The music Martin was listening to was interrupted. "The radio said [there were] tornado warnings for Ogle County," he said. The sky got darker, and rain began to pour down. "We could barely see out the windows," said Martin, who then saw something odd. "We saw Tom Taylor throw down his motor bike and run for the cafeteria exit door," he said. "We thought this was strange."

Tom wasn't the only one to leave his vehicle. John Bell, then sixteen, was on the back of a friend's motorcycle. "We went around the back of the school, trying to beat the long line of cars," he said. "When we came around the corner, the funnel cloud was coming toward us. We ditched the cycle and ran around the building."

Then, the fury of the tornado struck. "We could not see the V tip on any tornado," Martin said. "Then the windshield started cracking all over the bottom, going up. When the cracks reached the top, all the windows blew out. The rain, roof tar and rocks, dirt, et cetera, came roaring through the car. Our books flew out the windows. We all hit the floor."

Martin, in the back seat with Glenn Kibby, grabbed the seat springs under the front seat. Arty LaBuy and Tom Powers crawled into the space under the dashboard of the Chevelle. Glenn asked to help him pull the seat over their heads. "I said no," Martin said. "I wasn't going to let go of the springs.

"A few minutes later, which seemed longer, the rain and wind stopped. I looked out the window and thought a bomb had hit the Rockford area and us." Martin recalled a "quiet stillness" for a few moments, then "the screaming of several girls in the car next to us." The scene on the north side of the school was horrible as the school buses were scattered everywhere.

"The buses had rolled over the tops of many cars," Martin said. "Many school bus windows were open and down. Small children picked up previously by the buses had arms and legs crushed when the buses rolled through the parking lots. Car roofs were down to the bottom of the windows. We tried to pull the doors open to get the girls out, [but] we couldn't get them open."

John Bell and his friend didn't make it into the building but were not injured. "When the storm was over, we stayed and helped with the injured and dead," he said. "We used doors for stretchers. I remember walking a long way and still seeing injured people."

Aneita Ann Hurley was on a bus, sitting in her usual spot in the front. She was waiting for her sister Donna when she and another bus rider started talking about how black the sky was getting, "and within seconds, it turned a horrible green and gray and the cloud was dropping out of the sky upon us," Aneita said. "There was a dead calm, then the sound of a train roaring and whistling in the distance. You could feel the pressure in your ears. We began to run back into the school, realizing it was a tornado forming above us."

When she and her friend got to the school, she saw her science teacher, Marvin Schuster, holding the door open, screaming, "Get back in the building!" Aneita and her friend grabbed the metal rail on the door, and she could feel herself being lifted.

"I could feel my feet leaving the ground but could do nothing but hang onto the door rail, the wind was so strong," she said. "I remember Mr. Schuster grabbing my wrist and pulling me into the building and screaming, 'Get between the lockers.' As I was crawling to the lockers, I felt my face and arms being pierced by a million needles. There was burning and stinging all over my skin."

Marty Prather was in John Walker's car, waiting their turn to leave via East Avenue. It was a warm Friday afternoon, and the line was long. Then something unusual happened. "As we pulled up to wait in line to get out of the parking lot, we saw a police car coming up to the end of East Avenue," Marty said. "We figured there was an accident or something or somebody was in trouble."

It was Police Captain Whalen, siren roaring, lights flashing, who then lurched to a stop in front of the line of cars and buses.

"We thought that was kind of strange," Marty said. "He jumped out of his car and started yelling at the people in the first car and went from car to car. Some kids were running to the high school, others were running to the cars behind them saying, 'A tornado is coming. Get to the high school!' Then we did; we jumped out of my friend's car."

Marty said the sky to the west had "ugly colors of gray, yellow, green and smoke."

They followed the others to the main gym entrance, on the east side of the gym, and sat on the floor of the hallway. "Everyone was sitting there with their heads between their knees, thinking the worst and wondering what the heck was going to happen," he said. "It got very quiet, and then you could just hear the wind noise—loud, really loud, like a locomotive. The sound was incredibly loud and seemed to last a long time. I would imagine it was all of four or five minutes."

While Marty was lucky enough to get into the school, countless others were on buses when it became clear that a disaster was imminent.

John Church, a seventh grader, and Dennis Norem, an eighth grader, were on the second bus in the line. They both boarded the Caledonia-bound bus at the junior high. Fully loaded with high school students, the bus was awaiting its turn to exit onto East Avenue.

The students noted how dark the sky had turned, and what happened next seemed logical, John recalled. "The bus driver told us to get off the bus and get into the school," John said. "I don't think anybody realized that it was right there on top of us and whether that was the right decision or not. I don't think anybody knows."

John recalled that he probably was sitting about halfway back on the bus and that, when he did exit, he didn't get very far. "When I got off of the bus, it didn't seem like I got very far before the storm caught me," he said.

John was knocked to the ground and recalled hearing debris hitting the bus and the bus windows breaking. "I don't know if the bus tipped at that point," he said. "I don't know. I do know, and I always even hesitate to say this because it sounds silly, [but] in my mind, I remember seeing buses rolling or going over the top of you. That just seems unbelievable."

He doesn't know what hit him, but he knows it crushed his hip and he couldn't move.

"I have no idea how long that I lay there," he said. "I was laying there in the mud, because a lot of that area was relatively new, so I'm laying there in the mud, and stuff was hitting me, and it was pouring rain. I tried to get up a few times until I thought that I had a broken leg. That's all I knew. I didn't know I had a crushed hip."

John was fortunate because he had nearly reached the high school and was rescued right away. "I was not one of those that was lying out in the field for a long period of time," he said.

Among the people who helped him get into the school was Tom Pederson from Caledonia. At first, John was taken to the gym. After he lay there in the dark for a while, his brother Greg found him, so his family knew he was OK.

Eventually, the gym was converted into the temporary morgue, and John was moved to the cafeteria. He was placed on a door or a cafeteria table, and then he and the makeshift stretcher were put on top of seats of a working school bus and taken to St. Anthony Hospital in Rockford.

"All of the windows and everything were broken out [of the bus], but whatever kind of vehicle they could get to run, they did," he said.

There were so many people at the hospital that he was placed on the floor, wearing a piece of masking tape attached to his forehead with his name. His parents, unaware of the storm at first, got to the hospital about 9:00 p.m.

John's injury was so severe that the doctors were unsure if he would live or survive surgery. He had lost blood, and doctors told him that his injury was similar to being hit by a baseball bat in the hip. Eventually, he had surgery and went through a long rehabilitation. He missed the rest of his seventh grade year and was home-schooled the next year.

"I do have a limp, and they did go in and do a hip replacement in 1990," he said.

However, he considers himself lucky because seven students on his bus, all from Caledonia, were killed that day. One, Bruce Lindley, was a good friend.

"I know Bruce was on the bus behind me," John said. "Whether he got off the bus or was in the process of getting off the bus, I don't know."

Dennis Norem said that there was just a "What's going on?" feeling when he saw the threatening weather and students running back toward the gym.

"A student from the bus in front of us came back to our bus and said to our driver, 'You'd better get the kids off the bus. There's a storm coming,'" Dennis said.

So the bus driver, Mrs. Biggins, turned off the bus's motor, and students began to exit. The bus was northwest of the school, so the bus riders had to go around the bus to safety.

"You had to go around the front of the bus to get to the side entrance of the gym," Dennis said. "And by that time, the clouds were just boiling over the top of the gym.

"I made it halfway to the high school, and basically, I was blown down onto the ground. I kind of tucked up into a ball because, with that wind, things started to hit me. And that's the last thing I remember at that point."

That's because something hit Dennis on his head and knocked him out.

"The next thing I remember is being inside the gymnasium and somebody shaking me or talking to me, saying, 'Are you all right?' I was walking around, obviously in shock," he said.

To this day, he does not know how he got into the building.

When he came to, he said it was like waking up from a dream. So he answered the question he was asked. "I said, 'Yeah, I think I'm all right.' But I could barely see, and I began to get a little woozy. I just didn't feel very good." Dennis estimated that he was out for thirty or forty minutes. When he did regain his senses, he was in the gym, which had become the temporary morgue. "I remember seeing piles of dead bodies," he said. "My memory is that it was the center of the gym."

Dirt had blown into his eyes, and he went to clean them up. "I remember going into one of the bathrooms near the gymnasium to try and wash out my eyes, and I couldn't really do it. There was so much garbage and debris," he said. "I remember looking at myself. I looked pretty bad. I had short hair, and all of the mud had formed as a cap on my head. My face was all blown up, and I had all of this dirt and stuff in my eyes. So I looked pretty pathetic."

After a while, he was helped to the cafeteria, where injured survivors were gathering until they could get transportation to a hospital. "There were people in the cafeteria who were determining who was the most critically injured, a triage, and they were using cafeteria tables to haul people to the buses or whatever transportation they could get."

Dennis got on a bus, which may have been the same one that John Church was on because it was missing windows as well. "There was a younger guy driving our bus, and he was a smoker, and there was no windshield on the front of the bus," he said. "He was trying to light a cigarette while going down the road, so he was having a terrible time trying to keep his cigarette lit."

There were about twenty injured people, mostly students, on the bus. Some were on tables that had been placed on top of the seats; these, Dennis said, were the most seriously hurt.

"I had a cut in the back of my head and all this dirt on me and an injury to my hand, which turned out to be not much," Dennis said.

When he got on the bus, two kids sat in front of him. "They were kids I had gone to school with from Caledonia for several years, Johnny Darmon and Tammy Stephenson," he said. "We were all in the eighth grade together. I said, 'Johnny, are you doing OK?'

"They both looked at me and said, 'Who are you?' They did not recognize me."

Dennis ended up at Rockford Memorial Hospital, where he was cleaned up and had his hand X-rayed and his scalp stitched. "They got all of the dirt out of my eyes, thank God," he said.

He reunited with his parents much later that night after an aunt and uncle found him at the hospital. When he finally got home that night, he heard what had happened on his bus—that seven students who rode his bus were killed.

"The two girls sitting behind me, Pam Haines and Phyllis Van Brocklin, both were killed," he said. "They got off the bus."

Teri (Turner) Keegan was in the fourth or fifth bus in the line waiting to exit onto East Avenue. Teri, fifteen, was a freshman, looking forward to the weekend. She was seated in the middle of three ("We were always three to a seat," she said), about halfway back in the bus. Then someone looked out the window and said, "There's a tornado."

Teri was not concerned. "I'm like, it's a really nice day, it's Friday night, you know we're going to go out tonight. What do you mean, tornado?" Then, bus driver Gilbert Julin said, "Get down and get your hands over your heads! It's a tornado!"

"I could remember thinking, 'What!' Right then, it was like the calm before the storm. It sucked every bit of air out of you. You could not breathe. Then the windows started popping....You could see them snapping in and popping out. Then the bus started to rock, and it was just very surreal. It was rocking, then rocking very violently, then we started rolling over and over and over."

Teri said that she tried to keep her head covered and think about relaxing. "Just go limp," she said. "Relax, roll with it, ride it out. Then it was done. It was just done."

She didn't move for a moment. Then people started crawling out of the bus.

One of those was Roxanne Wearmouth, who said the bus landed upside down. She had to crawl over one of her friends, who had been killed, to get out of the bus. Roxanne had to be carried to the school and then was placed on a door and taken to Swedish-American Hospital in Rockford on a truck. She had a broken leg and ankle, and her eyes were swollen shut.

"My recollection was that we crawled up to get out of the window," Teri said. "Everybody was hurt. One of the girls with me had broken her back. There were moans, but you were in a self-preservation mode. You were scared, and you had to get out of there. You had heard of tornadoes, but what was a tornado? You knew, but you couldn't even comprehend the devastation."

So she and the other survivors left the bus. "Of course, we had no shoes," she said. "There must be a place somewhere with millions of shoes in it." That made her walk to the nearby school difficult because the storm had ripped up the driveway, recently paved with pea gravel. "I remember thinking that this is really going to hurt walking across this thing," Teri said. "There were kids running for the school; there were kids that couldn't run for the school."

Once the tornado hit, Marty Prather said he heard people crying. He and others went to the door to see what had happened. What he saw was out of a nightmare.

"The whole parking lot was cars turned over, cars on top of cars," he said. "The worst sight was when we opened the doors for the kids that didn't make it inside."

Many students ran to the shelter of the high school but found that the tremendous pressure of the storm had sealed the doors shut. "When we opened the door and saw all of these kids, you didn't know who they were because there was all this gravel and asphalt on their skin and clothes and face and hair. We didn't know what to tell them but to get inside. Of course, some didn't move at all because they were probably in shock. Some were sitting down. They were hurt. Others were just standing or sitting or crying. Some of us ran into the parking lot, and when you looked over to the west, you could see the whole subdivision was gone. All of the houses and trees and wires were down.…It was just…a total disaster."

Then he looked north and saw the buses. "The buses were all on their backs, some on their sides, like they had been rolled over several times," he said. "Myself and a couple of other guys went out into the parking lot and told kids to get inside. As we got farther out in the grass area where the buses were, there were kids sitting there crying. You didn't know if they were hurt or scared. Some of them were little kids, and we could just pick them up and carry them in. For other kids, it would take two of us to carry."

After Marty and others had carried in three or four kids, someone, probably a teacher or custodian, said, "We're taking doors off of the classrooms. Use them as stretchers for anybody that can't walk." So they grabbed doors and used them to carry injured children to shelter.

"There were a lot of kids out there," Marty said. "As many kids that did die, it was surprising that more didn't."

By this time, word of the disaster had spread, and family and friends were converging on the high school. "You couldn't drive up there, but there were parents who were running to the school, across the field, and they're saying, 'Marty! Have you seen my daughter? Have you seen my son?'"

As they carried in injured children, Marty said someone at the door told them where to go. "Take them into the gymnasium. Take them to the library or the cafeteria. There were a lot of people in the cafeteria."

It wasn't until later that Marty learned the gym was serving as an emergency morgue. "Somebody came up later, it could have been a half hour, and said not to go into the gym. We said, 'We've got two people we've taken in there and we've got another one.' And they said, 'Well, don't go into the gym because that's the morgue.'"

Suddenly, he realized what was going on. "We're like, 'What?' The kids that we took in there…the person who told us to take them in there knew that they were already dead! Of course, there were no lights, so once you opened the door, you could take somebody in there, but when the door was shut, there was no electricity, no light."

Celestia Matheson drove the last bus in line, No. 33, that day. Sensing a storm was coming, Celestia told the students to shut the windows. Then, recognizing that it was a tornado, she said, "I told the kids to open the windows and get down as low as they could under the seats. We just sat there and waited our turn."

Torn between crouching for safety and watching the approaching devastation, she lifted her head above the dashboard. What she saw was horrifying. "I could see other buses going into the air. I watched them turn in the air and land. I was partway down but also watching, and I knew that our bus was going to be one of those. So I started to get down when our bus went.…I went headfirst into the stairwell, which knocked me out."

When she regained consciousness, the bus was atop a car and she was on one of her riders. "Get off me! Get off me!" the little girl said. "That's what woke me up." The little girl, Penny (Pearse) Small, became a friend of Celestia's. The bus rolled over three times, its back wheels lodged on a car. Some of the boys on the bus got the doors open and helped younger students get to the high school. "I got a broken nose; it was crooked," she said. "They didn't put a cast on it, just straightened it."

Although the bus was full, no one was seriously injured. "And no one was killed on my bus," she said. Celestia doesn't know if she made the right decisions to have the students open the bus windows, to have her riders crouch down and not to leave the bus to seek shelter in the high school. "I don't know whether it was better to get out of the bus and go into the schoolhouse," she said. "Maybe we could have done that. I don't know. This is what I did."

One of the youngest bus survivor stories comes from Kathleen J. Boyd, who was a seven-year-old first grader at Washington School that day. "Fortunately, I was on one of the buses that had to make a drop off of children at Greenview Estates before we went to the high school," she said. "The bus driver, Larry Steinke, drove back into town on Newburg Road, down Locust to Pleasant and then to the junior high to head up Pearl Street to go to the high school. When we turned the corner onto Pearl, Larry stopped the bus and told us all to get under the seats. I looked up the street toward Pacemaker, and there was the most horrible thing. I can remember it as vivid today as I did that day. It is not something you easily forget."

After the tornado passed, the driver continued the bus journey toward the high school, "turning from street to street to avoid downed power lines," Boyd said. "My dad got me off the bus at Fifth Street somewhere. How he found the bus is beyond me."

At the same time, Leslie Wright, then a fifteen-year-old sophomore at Belvidere High School, was in Circle Drive in a blue-and-white Chevrolet station wagon with two friends. They were waiting for another friend, Carla. All of a sudden, another girl jumped into the back seat. It was Judi Ford, the daughter of Leslie's favorite English teacher. (Ford went on to become Miss America in 1969.) "I don't recall why she was there," Leslie said, wondering if she had jumped in to take shelter from the sudden downpour.

Soon enough, they spotted Carla, struggling with two armfuls of books, her clarinet case and gym clothes. As they watched her walk to the car, the sky turned strangely dark and the gusting winds and driving rain pushed and pulled at her. Carla turned back and disappeared into the building, Leslie said.

Then the storm hit. The sound of hail hitting the roof and hood was deafening, Leslie recalled. As the car began to rock and sway, Leslie wondered if it was going to flip over. "I remember yelling the obvious out loud: 'Put your heads down!' Head pressed into my lap with my arms wrapped tightly around, I had no idea what was happening. A bad storm for sure."

When the pressure blew out the side windows, the station wagon rocked more ferociously. Then, calm.

"Unsure of what had just happened, we got out of the car and made our way to the school," Leslie said. "I vaguely remember looking out toward the grass fields to the east and seeing yellow buses scattered. And at the entrance, I recalled twisted aluminum door frames."

Chapter 6

HEROES CAME IN ALL SIZES

To this day, Roger Wheeler says he can't remember what the tornado looked like, even though he saw it with his own eyes. What he can remember is how fast he ran from outside the north end of the high school to get to the gym.

"Ollie Benzel would have been proud of how fast I ran," Roger said about the gym teacher. "With the wind at my back, my strides were getting quite long. I remember that because I thought to myself that I have to be careful not to fall."

Roger entered the hallway on the east side of the school that separates the gym from the main building and held open the door for others. Soon, he had the same problem others had in holding open the door. "Very soon, it was getting difficult for those to even stand up," Roger said. "I heard the crashing of glass, and the wind got very strong in the hallway. While holding onto the door handle, I looked out to see the buses rolling and bouncing across the field to the north. I knew my sister and friends were on those buses."

With the glass on the doors shattered, the wind rushed through the opening and down the hallways. "The wind in the hallway got more intense," Roger said. "I moved into the building, hollering, 'Get down! Get down!' A young girl was 'bouncing' toward the door—the wind was really strong—I reached out, grabbed her arm, pulled her down and lay on top of her. The wind got even more intense. I believed I would die. I thought of my mom and dad. I saw them in my mind and told them not to be sad, that this was OK."

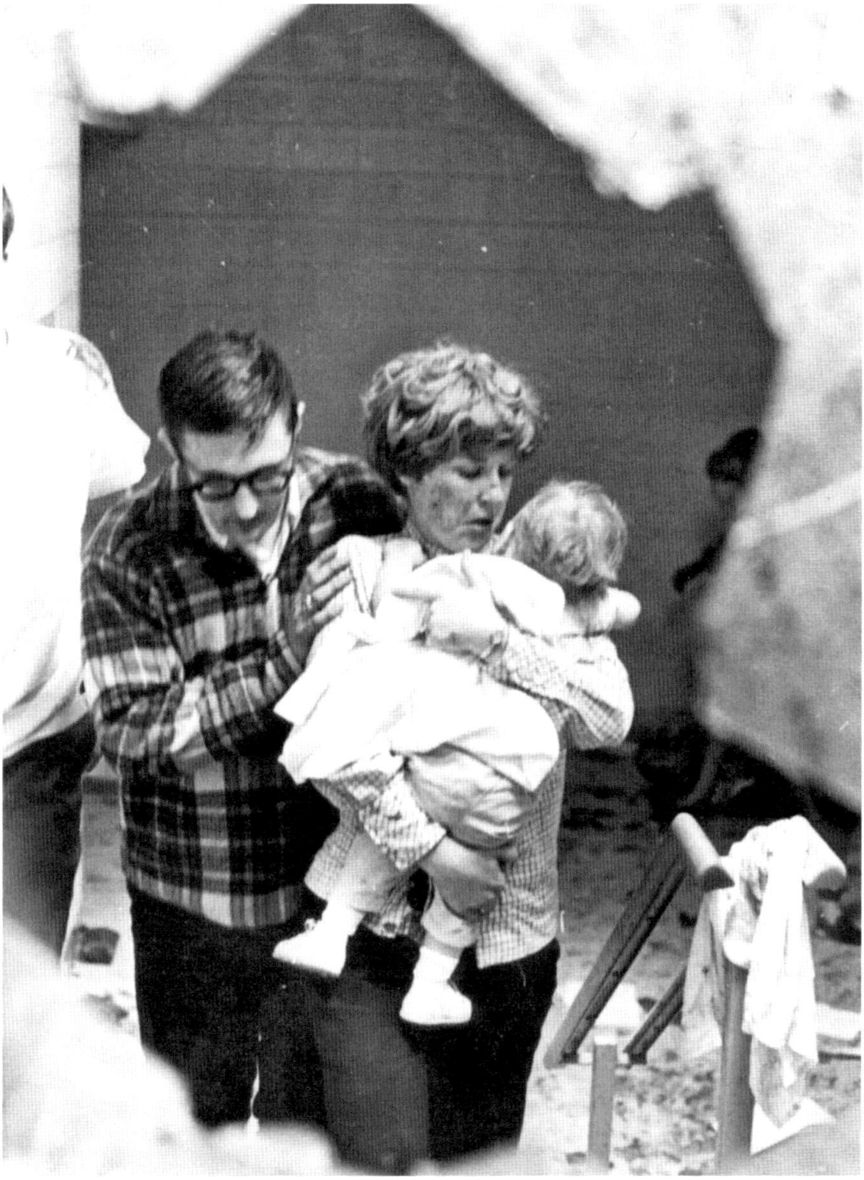

This photo, taken through an opening in broken glass, shows a young family comforting one another at Belvidere High School. *Courtesy of Boone County Historical Museum.*

The wind got calmer and finally stopped. Roger looked up to see people moving toward the school, people who all looked the same. They were stunned and covered in mud.

Three Belvidere High School students, one wearing his letterman's jacket, help with the cleanup effort at the school. *Courtesy of Boone County Historical Museum.*

The roof of the Immanuel Lutheran School gym has been partially torn away. *Courtesy of Boone County Historical Museum.*

"I jumped up, and almost immediately, there were battleship gray people crawling and walking into the hallway…those that had not made it inside," he said. "Cathy Nelson yelled to me that she had a young girl that couldn't see. I lifted the girl up and took her into the gym and laid her down. We initially made the gym as a place to put those that were badly hurt. Sometime later, I noticed this girl looked at me when she heard my voice. That was a good sign."

THE GYM GETS A GRIM NEW ROLE

The school, traditionally a safe place, seemed to have been spared from the tornado's destruction, despite its loss of doors and windows.

Fred Brereton, former mayor of Belvidere, who was a member of Coach Joe Lewis's baseball team that was scheduled to play at Freeport that day, found out it wasn't so safe after all. The report of bad weather caused the game to be cancelled, so the team practiced in the gym.

"Doug Gorham and I were playing catch to warm up when the gym lights went out," Fred said. "Because of the skylights in the gym, there was still enough light to continue to warm up. Coach Lewis told us to sit along the bleachers by the wall. We thought we had a few minutes more to warm up, when he returned to the gym with a stern voice, saying, 'I told you guys to get over by the bleachers!'"

Fred recalled that there was something in his voice that meant business. As the players got to the bleacher area and sat on the floor, they all looked up. "The roof on the gym began to flex, and hailstones came crashing through the skylights," Brereton said. "The pressure in our ears began to fill up, and we knew this was a severe storm. Fearing the roof might collapse, we all headed for the hallway. Once in the hallway, all hell broke loose. I dove for cover and began to pray."

The girl whom Roger Wheeler had rescued and others who had been injured were moved from the gym to the cafeteria. "Eventually, it was questioned whether the gym roof was safe, since during the tornado, it was noticed that the roof was bouncing up and down," he said. "Because of this, the living were transferred to the cafeteria, and the gym became the morgue."

Fred said that after the roar of the storm died down there was "an eerie silence….As we stood up, there was a car on its side against the doors at the end of the hallway. Then, students began to enter the building. Our best friends were barely recognizable because of the thick mud covering them from head to foot, all in a state of shock."

Once Malvina (Hart) Lutz, who had survived the tornado in a car in Circle Drive, got to the door, she followed others who headed toward the gym, where wrestling mats were on the floor. "Everyone ran to them, crouched down on their hands and knees and covered our heads with our arms," she said. "It was dark. Everyone was crying or praying out loud. I don't remember noise as much as a vacuum feeling. My ears were popping. Once the group of people I was with realized it must be over, we cautiously started checking ourselves over. We were wet and dirty. I found a Kleenex in my raincoat pocket. I passed it on to someone who needed it more."

For a few moments, the group of survivors sat stunned. This was before cellphones. The school had lost electricity, and they were in a dark hallway. "Then a door on the side wall opened," Malvina said. "Students started pouring in from [where] the buses [were]. The looks on their faces were [of] sheer terror."

Doors Become Stretchers

Leslie Wright described a similar scene once she got into the school. "Inside, bewildered school kids and teachers began to realize the impact of the storm," she said. "Soon, streams of kids who had been walking home began returning to the school, covered with dirt and mud. My friend Kay's face was a mud mask."

Driver education teacher Jim Barr rode out the storm in a locker bay and then returned to the front door, which he had been forced to abandon because of the fierce wind and destruction. When he got there, he saw a student come in from another door. "She was covered with blood and black with mud. She said—and I can still remember this—'It's a complete disaster out there.'"

Jim looked to the northwest toward the baseball field and saw several buses. "Some were upside down….My stomach did a flip-flop….I just visualized those buses being picked up off the ground."

Jim then set to the task of setting up aid for the survivors in the library, cafeteria and gym. "They had to put some mats up to make a wall in the gym," he said. "They put those beyond help back there."

The snow that fell on April 23, 1967, covers desks and other classroom items at Immanuel Lutheran School. *Courtesy of Boone County Historical Museum.*

No one knows who first thought of removing doors to use as stretchers, but soon, many were helping out, including William Johnson and Orrie Halverson, a math teacher. In a 1997 interview with the *Rockford Register Star*, Orrie said that he, Jim Barr and a student helped in a rescue.

"There were three of us," Orrie said. "We pulled two cars apart, kind of picked up the back end of a car and shoved it over. A senior girl was pinned in the middle of them. We asked if she was OK. She said, 'Yup,' and got up and ran away."

Shortly after the storm ended, Aneita Ann Hurley, who was in the locker bay, recalled hearing teachers tell everyone to go to the library for safety. The library was in the middle of the first floor of the building and had a sunken floor. This was the main gathering place for survivors to find siblings and parents and for parents to find their children. Aneita began to look for her sister. "I was screaming her name, 'Donna! Donna!' Then a teacher calmed me down and said Donna was OK," she said.

From behind, Aneita heard her sister Donna call her name. "She grabbed me, and we had to wait there for our parents to get us to take us home," Aneita said.

"As more students came into the school, adults started taking charge," Malvina Lutz said. "We were told to go back the way we came, keep going down the hall and into the sunken library. Able-bodied men were being asked to take down doors to help carry the wounded and dead. The gymnasium would be used as the morgue."

Malvina was in a group that made its way up the stairs and down the hall, past the main entrance. She noticed that—incredibly—the hallway windows were intact.

But she was shocked at what she saw through the glass on her right. "What I saw when I looked out to the west was unbelievable," she said. "Everything was gone. All the houses were down to rubble, the cars in the Circle Drive were crushed, upside down. It looked like Belvidere was gone. As bad as that was, I am thankful that I did not turn and look the other direction toward the buses. Many of my friends from the junior high were among the bus riders."

In a short time, the library began to fill with survivors, many of them leaving bloody footprints on the floor.

"The lights were out, but once the storm passed, the sky got lighter," Malvina said. "Some natural light was filtering into the library. So many people of all ages were coming into the library. It didn't take long for me to get separated from the family I had arrived with. I started seeing my friends from the buses come into the library. They were even dirtier and wetter, and most had no recognition of friends. They were all in shock."

The rescue effort at the high school was coolly efficient. The *Rockford Register-Republic* reported that students and teachers who had been in the school started rescue attempts immediately. In addition to doors, cafeteria tables were also used as stretchers.

Orrie recalled that a couple of kids ran down to the Green Giant plant "and got a couple of end loaders to start moving debris and cars. I wouldn't have thought of that."

Marge Hinrichs noted that the same boys who were usually troublesome were quick to respond. "Some of the boys…unbelievable…they were rascals to their name, but they took the doors off their hinges and picked up the people," she said. "They put people on those doors and carried them into the building."

As she waited in the library, Malvina recalled that another call went out for more men "to come help with the hurt children outside."

There was a warning not to light matches or lighters because no one was sure that the gas line was intact. "Another request," she said, "was for someone to go into the girls' bathrooms and take out the sanitary napkins to use as bandages."

Roger Wheeler started to go outside to help when he was distracted by "a gal hollering, 'Get me out of here.'" The girl had been caught on the push rail of the door, which had had all of it glass blown out. "Against her was a bed mattress," Roger said. "And against that a car laying on its side....She didn't seem to be hurt badly."

When he got outside, he saw utter destruction. "It was bad," he said. "By this time, some doors had been taken off of classrooms and were being used as stretchers. There were a lot of people in the field. I went out there. There were many sights I wish not to describe. I looked for those [survivors who] showed signs of life to try to help. There wasn't much we could do for them except get them off the field."

Some vehicles were showing up by now. A path had been cleared for them to get close, and some were leaving for hospitals directly from the field.

Among those waiting in the library for their parents were three Fowler children: Cheryl Sturges, then a high school freshman, and her brother Craig and sister Connie. Another sister, Cindy, a seventh grader, was at confirmation class at Zion Lutheran Church.

Cheryl described the scene in the library as one of many young people crying and hugging. She recalled hugging her siblings. "Once I found them, I didn't want to let them go anywhere," said Cheryl, who recalled telling them to stay put. "I was almost acting like a mother figure," she said. So the three sat and waited.

"We were sitting there, wondering why our parents had not come after us," Cheryl said. "We lived five miles south of town, and I kept saying, 'We'll be OK.' We sat there, huddled together." Then, somehow, her sister Cindy found them in the library. "I don't know how she got there," Cheryl said. It was close to 6:00 p.m. when a neighbor took the Fowlers and others home. When they got home, they learned that their parents hadn't known about the tornado until well after it had passed.

"It was such a major storm, but yet five miles away, they had no idea what hit Belvidere," she said. "They said they tried to get to town about five o'clock. They came over the tollway and saw the devastation, but by then, the roads were all blocked off, and they weren't letting anyone come in. So they figured the best thing to do was to go home."

By this time, worried parents were beginning to arrive on the scene. Roger said, "I had a few ask me if I had seen their child. It was hard to say no, but to go look in the library or cafeteria. I could see the distress on their faces, and I could not settle that."

Aneita realized that by deciding not to walk home because of the storm and to accept a ride from a friend, she had broken her daily routine. She had never been to the high school, so why would her parents look for her there? "How was I going to find my way home?" she said. "My parents wouldn't know where I was."

After what "seemed like an eternity," Aneita's father arrived at the library. As they made their way through the building, she heard someone call her name.

"I stopped and turned to see my best friend, Linda Shue, leaning against the wall," Aneita said. "She was so covered with mud, straw, grass and blood that I didn't recognize her until she started talking to me. I stayed by her until my dad found her mother. She was a survivor."

The BHS library once anchored the main classroom building on the first floor. It had glass walls and steps down to the floor with entrances from each of the main corridors on the first floor. Surrounded by the building, it had no windows. So when school librarian Marge Hinrichs heard that a tornado was coming, she didn't believe the news delivered by another staff member.

"I could never see outside, so I always kind of joked and said, 'Well, I'd never know if a tornado was coming or not,'" Marge said. "Yeah, I thought she was teasing me. And she said, 'No, Marge, I mean it.'"

Marge ran up the steps, went into the hallway by the main office and stood against the wall. Suddenly, she saw teacher Charlie Harned running down the hall. "Oh, my God," he said. "The buses have overturned." Then the doors flew open, and corn shucks and other debris blew in.

Marge ran to the front door, where the first person she saw was a young girl "with her nose almost cut off," she said. "We gathered up the little ones and put them against the wall. They were dirty and they were crying and they were hurt and they wanted mommy and they didn't want Miss Hinrichs," she said. "It was very, very sad. They gathered everybody in the library that was able to be gathered."

Principal Virgil McAllister had a bullhorn, and as the parents came to pick up their children or look for them, he shouted their names, Marge said.

In the absence of electricity, a bullhorn had become the school's public address system.

"The library was big but filled up quickly," Malvina (Hart) Lutz said. "As time went by, adults began arriving from outside. They would enter the library on the stair landing and call out for loved ones. I couldn't believe it when I saw my Uncle Frank! He was yelling for his daughter, Bonnie. I ran up to him, but he was so frantic to find Bonnie that he left me standing there and went on looking.

"More and more people came into the library. And then, my mom and dad were standing there calling for me! How did they know I was there? I ran to them and had a very emotional reunion."

Malvina's cousin Bonnie did survive. A senior, she was in the parking lot in an old Volkswagen Beetle when the tornado hit.

But others weren't as fortunate to find their loved ones right away.

The Last to Leave

The last one to leave the high school the night of April 21, 1967, was assistant principal Joan Brannah. Normally, her day ended at 3:40 p.m. when the final bell rang, but that day, larger forces intervened.

Just before 3:50 p.m., Joan glanced outside the front windows to see how the end-of-day exodus was progressing and saw a slate-colored sky to the west. Alarmed, she ran into the front hall, where she and others flattened themselves against a wall.

"I looked up and saw the doors to the gym, and almost in slow motion, I watched the glass crack and fall," she said. "Then, all of a sudden, everything hit."

Once the storm passed, she helped to herd survivors into the library and found herself stunned by the condition of those who had been outside when the tornado hit. "They had this kind of zombie look," Joan said. "It looked like they had been dipped in chocolate. It was the strangest thing. All you could see was the whites of their eyes showing."

In a matter of moments, Joan became the lead administrator on the scene. Virgil McAllister—though a respected and experienced principal—had difficulty coping with the scope of the tragedy. "It hit him hard," Joan said. "He had been in the navy in World War II, and we called him 'sir.' But he went to pieces. It was too much for him. He was overwhelmed. So I wound up taking charge."

In an article in the *Rockford Register-Republic*, a reporter wrote about approaching Principal McAllister outside the building. "I can't talk…I can't talk…" he said, bursting into tears as he buried his head in his hands and returned to the building.

Joan stayed at the high school until she was ordered to leave. "I was the last one there," she said. "The National Guard came in and said that I needed to leave then."

A Heroic Decision

Eugene Wille was the junior pastor at Immanuel Lutheran Church in 1967. At that time, the church was located on Boone Street, north of the Kishwaukee River, while the church's school was south of the river at 8525 East Second Street, a short distance northwest of Belvidere High School. The school and church are in the same location now on Second Street.

On the afternoon of April 21, 1967, after Pastor Wille and his wife had driven to a farm on Wheeler Road to pick up some eggs, he dropped his wife off at their home on West Lincoln Avenue and headed for the school, where he had a 4:00 p.m. appointment with a confirmation class.

Pastor Wille and the senior pastor, Arnold Guerke, each had confirmation classes with public school students that day—Guerke had the eighth graders, Wille the seventh graders.

While driving back from their egg run, the Willes noticed that the southwest sky had turned gray. As Pastor Wille arrived at the school about 3:45 p.m., he looked up again at the sky.

"I could see what was building up," he said. "It looked very stormy. As I got out of the car and ran to the front doors, the thing that scared me was the sound. That's the first thing I remember—the roar, the sound of trains above the school, from the sky."

Pastor Wille won't forget what he saw when he looked up. "There was a mass of rolling, black swirling clouds, descending with destruction, coming down right behind the school. It dawned on me: TORNADO! You knew *that* was a tornado."

Pastor Wille ran into the school and—amazingly—found no one. He did see someone in the hallway, who said, "Downstairs. Everyone's in the basement." Pastor Wille ran to the bottom of the stairs to a small supply room, where he found Pastor Guerke and Joel Schumacher, the acting principal.

Police captain Francis "Dutch" Whalen commands attention in the lobby of the gym of Belvidere High School. His warnings prior to the tornado are credited with saving lives. *Courtesy of Boone County Historical Museum.*

Pastor Wille wasn't the only person to be surprised to find the school empty. Naomi Schultz left work at First National Bank in downtown Belvidere and drove to Immanuel Lutheran School to pick up her nine-year-old daughter Debbie for a dental appointment. "When I got there, things were quiet," Naomi says. "I got into the building and could see activity at the other end of the hallway. Somebody yelled, 'There's a storm coming. Get to the basement and go to the locker room and into the showers.'"

"All the kids were in the shower rooms and the locker rooms," Pastor Wille said. "They had been placed there by their teachers, and the teachers knew a storm was imminent."

But Naomi didn't go straight downstairs. "We had just bought a new car—it was a Pontiac Tempest—the first new car since we were married," she said. "And I couldn't let anything happen to it. So I calmly walked back to the car to roll the windows up. After I did that, I turned around and saw the roof come off of the hospital. I hurried back into the building. I ran into a teacher, and she said, 'RUN!'"

Naomi assumed her daughter was in the basement. "When I got [there], she said, 'Mama!' There were teachers there, and they started us singing," Naomi said.

The song? "Jesus Loves Me," Pastor Wille said.

As the children sang—less than a minute after Pastor Wille arrived—the storm hit. "We heard the regular school bell go off, then one of the after-school bells," he said. "Then we heard some of the damage upstairs, you know, the crashing and smashing of glass above us. Then, maybe after a minute of silence, we thought maybe we were in the eye of it, so we thought we'd better wait another minute or so."

Naomi had a similar experience. "We heard everything happen," she said. "We were trying to increase the volume [of the singing] when the roof blew off the gym. The noise got louder…like lots of trains rolling on top of us. There was a calm, but we knew the sound would be back, and it was. The second time around, it was a little harder to get the kids singing.

"Some [children] were whimpering. We just prayed. I prayed that, if I died, I hoped it would be quick. I covered my daughter's head. I thought, 'This is it.' They kept us down there for a little bit before things got organized."

In retrospect, Naomi Shultz recalled this anecdote: "My daughter pointed out that we were good Lutherans. The girls went to the girls' shower, the boys to the boys' shower."

That's where second grader Phil Beu was that day. "We went into the boys' locker room, which was in the basement," he said. "It was kind of devastating to look up and see the sky when we came upstairs."

Phil and his classmates were worried about the fate of their class project. They were raising a chicken from an egg.

"After the tornado, we were concerned and wanted to know if the chicken had survived," Phil said. "Our teacher told us she found the chicken alive on top of the rubble. His name was Fluffy."

When the tornado seemed to be over, those inside opened the door and walked up into the gymnasium. "The first thing we saw was the sky, the clouds. The southern part of the gym roof was all gone," Pastor Wille said. "There we were, dazed and amazed."

The church officials checked out the school to assess the damage and look for anyone who had survived. While there was no loss of life, they found the damage to be severe. Three of the four classrooms in the corner were gone.

"The roof was gone, and the outside walls were gone," Pastor Wille said. "Two of those three rooms had just been built a few months before and had yet to be officially dedicated, but we were using them. They were gone and the contents scattered."

As the school leaders looked around, they saw that one of the walls in the kindergarten room had caved in. There were broken windows and water-soaked items. Cars were scattered in the teachers' parking lot, including Martha Collins's Volkswagen Beetle, which had been tossed the farthest away. Speaking of cars, Naomi noted from her survivor's perspective how absurd it had been to be worried about hers. "My car? Oh, all the windows were blown out, and it was badly scratched," she said. "I stop and think now how materialistic I was. By then, my car didn't bother me one bit."

Although the storm killed seventeen children, only one student from Immanuel Lutheran was lost, seven-year-old Becky Vogelsang. She was killed on a bus at the high school.

The fact that no one else was lost is the result of quick thinking by the man whom Pastor Wille considers the unsung hero of the tornado.

Becky was on the first bus to leave Immanuel Lutheran, which had an enrollment of about 240 students from kindergarten to eighth grade. Many of the other students had been picked up by parents, which left about 80 students waiting for the second bus.

Most of those students were waiting outside the school in the playground when the acting principal, Joel Schumacher, sensed danger in the air and ordered everyone inside. "He said, 'Teachers, get your kids inside,'" Pastor Wille said. "Some of the teachers were inside already. And some of the teachers suggested that they send the kids to their classrooms. They said, 'That's where the teachers are; they'll be fine.'"

But Joel was adamant. "He insisted that they all go down to the basement," Pastor Wille said. "And the teachers followed his orders, and they all went down to the basement, into the locker rooms, where they were safe."

In a story from the *Rockford Morning Star*, Joel's wife said, "My husband is very storm-conscious, and he was sure something bad was coming. He and the other teachers got the children inside, and the other male teacher, Thomas McGhee, started them singing to take their minds off the storm."

Pastor Wille knows that Joel's quick actions saved lives.

"Had they gone to their respective classrooms, there is no doubt that many of these kids would have been injured, if not killed," he said. "Some of those classrooms were directly hit and hugely damaged.

"He was determined, whether it was insight or a sense of some impending disaster. You don't know if it's a bad rainstorm or something else, but he sensed it was a big one."

Looking back, Pastor Wille believes Joel was a hero, though not recognized as such at the time.

Chapter 7

A BUILDING STANDS STRONG

When Bill and Barbara Hammond drove home from work from Genoa to Belvidere with several co-workers, they were forced to find an alternate route into the city because Genoa Road was blocked. As they drove around and to the west, they spotted signs of a serious storm.

"The electrical poles along the road were bent to the north," Barbara said, "some of them leaning way out over the road, but still I had not thought of a tornado having hit…just high winds. The clouds were still low and seemed to be just over our heads."

They cut across and approached Belvidere from the west, spotting more damage. "A two-story brick house stood with its roof gone," she said. "Electrical lines were lying in the road. It began to penetrate that just high winds couldn't have wrought the destruction."

Then they got to the scene on Logan Avenue, east of the city, and DeWane's Restaurant and Auction Barn. Among the things they saw were a cow standing in a field close to the road, black with mud. "There was a little white on her underside and her wide, frightened eyes were the only white on her body," Barbara said. "A car was lying on its top with the lights still on and men pulling at the doors. A man with a baby under his arm ran to a car. Semis were lying on their sides, a twisted mess of metal."

She also remembers the implement dealers across Logan Avenue, where "heavy equipment was tipped and scattered like toys abandoned by a bored child."

DeWane's Restaurant and Auction Barn. *Courtesy of Ray DeWane.*

The counter and stools are ready for customers, but the roof is gone at the Milk-E-Way Donut shop, located west of DeWane's on Logan Avenue. *Courtesy of Boone County Historical Museum.*

Belvidere North High School students paint a mural at C&H Cabinet Gallery on Logan Avenue, former site of DeWane's Restaurant and Auction Barn. *Courtesy of Troy Yunk.*

Bill was driving with Barbara, along with seven female co-workers catching a ride home with them. "By this time, [the women] were all sobbing and Bill was talking a steady stream," recalled Barbara. "The skating rink on the corner where we usually came into town was demolished—bent and twisted steel framework is about all that was left. A small donut shop on the south side of the street was gone except for the counter and stools and internal fixtures. In other words, the walls and roof were completely gone. The houses on the north side of the street seemed battered but in one piece."

The farther the Hammonds drove west into town, the lesser the damage. As they dropped off their passengers, they noticed that electrical lines were lying on Fremont Street near Fourth. One of the Hammonds' passengers jumped out of the car before anyone could stop her and ran to her nearby house. "We waited until she was safely inside," Barbara said. Then, as the couple turned around, it started to rain "real hard" and "the winds started blowing, so much it was almost horizontal. There were trees and wires all over, but we got her home."

While the northwest side of Belvidere was generally spared, that wasn't true to the east and southeast. One Belvidere landmark not spared from the tornado's wrath was DeWane's Restaurant and Auction Barn on Logan Avenue, which began business in 1930.

April 21, 1967, was "sale day," said Ray DeWane, then the business's owner/operator. The sign on the wooden front of the steel building said it all: "Livestock Exchange Auction Every Friday."

"We sold anything with four legs—cattle, hogs, sheep, horses. That day we didn't have any horses," Ray said.

There were dozens of people in the restaurant and sale barn; the parking lot had more than one hundred cars. "It was a typical Friday," Ray said, "until about ten minutes to four."

That's when Dr. Elmer Strathman, the veterinarian for the auction house, had some urgent news.

"He went to leave," Ray said. "He was done for the day, testing cattle and vaccinating hogs. Well, he's originally from Kansas, and he knows what tornadoes are like. He came in and told my brother, Larry, our auctioneer, that there was a very bad storm coming and everybody should take precautions and get into a safe place."

"We ran inside screaming like banshees, and everyone ran down the stairs," Dr. Strathman said in a *Rockford Register Republic* article. "All of the seats were filled when we announced it, and everybody picked up and got into a safe place," Ray said. Most of the people took shelter against a wall on the lower level, while restaurant customers ducked behind the counter.

Ray saw the storm strike three machinery dealers across the road. He watched combines crushed as easily as if they were flimsy toys. "It was like taking a piece of paper and crumpling it in your hand," he said. "I watched [the tornado] go across the road. It hit us head on."

The tornado tore through DeWane's parking lot and smashed into the building, slicing off part of the roof and destroying the twenty-four-hour restaurant and the chutes and staging areas in the rear of the building.

"It tore off all of the sheds," Ray said. "Thank God for that steel Butler building. It's still out there today. The steel part of it stood, but the rest blew away."

When it did, it took the life of Harold Gustafson, who worked in the chutes in the back. Harold actually had found shelter with another veterinarian, Dr. James Harvey; the two huddled together, but the storm spared James, leaving him with only a broken wrist.

"Harry didn't have a blemish on him," Ray said. "The doctor at the hospital said that there are times when the air just gets sucked out of your lungs."

At least one hundred cars and trucks were damaged that day, Ray said, but he and Harry Wennmacher got one to work and took Harold to the hospital, where he was pronounced dead. Another death occurred at DeWane's when a group of women pulled their car into its parking lot. Mary Hamre, who was returning home from Dundee, was killed when debris was blown into the car.

A woman was severely injured in the front section of the building and taken to a hospital in a station wagon. Also, a man and another woman were seriously injured in front of the auction house when their car was blown off the road.

"If that doctor hadn't warned us, we were probably dead meat," Ray said. "I'm sure there would have been [more deaths]. I don't know how we escaped. We had those big windows. It blew everything out of there."

Although cattle were scattered and trucks tipped over, Ray said they lost only two cows. He added that the Freeport Sheriff's Association brought horses and rounded up the stray cattle.

In one of the first indications of Belvidere's resiliency, DeWane's held its weekly auction the next Friday, April 28. "We never missed a sale date," Ray said. "We had some people come in and help get us set up. We were running short of capacity and lot in livestock, but we did have our sale the next week."

That doesn't mean it was easy. They ran the business out of a house trailer for a year, Ray said. DeWane's continued operating until it closed in 1987 after fifty years in business. The steel building that withstood the tornado still stands and is the home of C&H Cabinet Gallery. It features a mural of the building's history, which was created by Belvidere North High School art teacher Troy Yunk and his students.

Chapter 8

A STRONG STORM TO THE END

When people recall the tornado and all of its impact, most of the interest centers on Chrysler, Pacemaker, Highland Hospital, the schools and the homes in the city.

But the tornado had enough energy left to destroy entire farms to the east, especially along Lawrenceville Road. Lawrenceville Road darts straight east out of Belvidere before coming to a T intersection at Garden Prairie Road.

Gary and Ann Turner had struggled as a young family but were able to buy 120 acres at 8109 Lawrenceville Road. Gary milked cows and farmed another 75 acres that belonged to his uncle Lloyd and did odd jobs to make a little extra money for his growing family. The Turners had two children, Paul and Amy, at Kishwaukee School in Garden Prairie, and a younger daughter, Sarah, who was not yet school age.

"Ann and I struggled when we farmed," Gary said. "We didn't have much money." But they had enough to put new carpeting into their old farmhouse.

That Friday, Gary was the only one home and was out repairing a fence to keep his young heifers on pasture and grass. Ann was shopping at the Piggly Wiggly in Belvidere; the two oldest Turner children were in school, while the youngest was at a friend's house.

"It was a nice warm day," he said. "It was April, and it was just so darn nice that I don't think I even had a jacket on. I was working the fence, and I saw some [dark] clouds up in the distance to the far west."

But they didn't look any different from those seen in the early spring storms that are common in northern Illinois, "so it didn't really concern me

Left: The Loveridge Farm northeast of Belvidere outside Garden Prairie sustained damage, including to this truck and silo. *Courtesy of Boone County Historical Museum.*

Below: Jim Turner (*left*) points to the new location of his house, while his father, Lloyd Turner (*right*), shows where the home stood before the tornado moved it that day. They are holding an aerial photo of the Turner Farm on Lawrenceville Road. *Courtesy of Jim Turner.*

too much," he said. Gary had run out of staples, the kind that nail barbed wire to the fence, so he realized he had to make a trip to the Farm & Fleet, located on Logan Avenue, east of Belvidere.

"It was like four in the afternoon, something like that," he said. "It wasn't time to milk the cows." The cows got milked about 5:30 p.m., so Gary knew he would have time to make a quick trip.

Gary got into his early 1960s blue Chevy half-ton pickup and headed west on Lawrenceville. He got less than a mile when he looked in the fields to the southwest and saw a big cloud of dirt.

"I actually never saw a funnel cloud," he said. "It was to the southwest of us, and it was rolling on the ground, and I was startled by it.

"Then, of course, life-changing events happened. I never thought about getting out of my truck. I thought the storm would be kind of narrow, so I put the truck in reverse and started back east."

Gary didn't realize the storm was as wide and menacing as it was; he figured he could outdrive it. So he started backing down the road, past his own place.

"I think hindsight's really good," he said. "I think I could have jumped out of my truck and ran somewhere, maybe found a hole to jump into, a basement or something. But I was concerned that I was in harm's way, and I just kept backing up the road."

Gary thought he was doing well, outrunning the storm. "I was really backing up pretty fast," he said. He passed the farm, a quarter mile from his house. Then, as he passed the Henninger farm on the south side of the road, he saw shingles and other objects flying out of the yard, "just taking off."

At this point, Gary quit driving. He knew the doors of the truck, a "clunker" he had picked up at a farm sale, wouldn't hold up, so he tried to duck under the dashboard, lest he get tossed out.

"So I went to throw myself down on the floor of the truck," he said. But he didn't make it. As he moved to the floorboard, the tornado tossed the truck like a toy, and Gary went crashing through the passenger window—face first. "I think the truck flipped completely over, and my head hit the window but my teeth hit the windowsill of the door frame."

Miraculously, the truck didn't tumble farther but got stacked up against a ten-inch-wide utility pole. Gary, still in the truck, was knocked out but doesn't know for how long.

"I can't judge it," he said. "But the more I think about it, [it was] longer than I thought. I didn't even realize I [had been] knocked out."

Gary got out of the truck and noticed how eerily quiet it was. "It was just as quiet as can be," he recalled. "There was no wind. I looked to the north, and it was just quiet. I didn't see any sign of the storm."

He looked at the nearby Pfluger farm and saw that the barn and other buildings were gone. So he started to walk down Lawrenceville Road, past his home, where he knew nobody was home, and went to the house of his uncle, Lloyd, who lived across the road.

"I walked up his driveway," he said. "His house was cockeyed, and his buildings, the barn buildings, were all blown away."

And there sat his uncle's car, the only damage a blown-out back window. Then, Gary's aunt and uncle came out of the basement, where they had sought shelter. Lloyd took one look at his nephew and said, "We'd better get you to the hospital."

Gary asked to be taken to Highland Hospital, where his wife was more likely to look for him than Belvidere's other hospital, St. Joseph's.

The two men drove into town and turned south on State Street past Manley Motors, where they saw a nurse stumbling up the street. "Her uniform was all dirty, and she had this blank stare on her face, and I said, 'That doesn't look good. We'd better go to St. Joe's,'" Gary said.

So they turned around and headed east to St. Joseph's, when, for the first time, Gary realized the extent of his injuries. "It was about then that I realized that my top teeth were gone," he said. "They just broke off. My teeth broke right off."

When the men got to St. Joseph's, Gary was taken into the emergency room, where Dr. Jim Ellis treated him. "I was basically the first patient—the first tornado victim—that went into St. Joseph's emergency room," Gary said. He got "fifty or sixty stitches" in his face, a face that was seen by many in newspaper accounts of his ordeal.

Meanwhile, Ann Turner, who had been grocery shopping, heard about the tornado and dashed home only to find she couldn't get there. "She got within a mile of the farm, and of course, the damaged road was closed with debris," Gary said. "She came running home, [and] when she got here, Mr. Ed Greves, who was a volunteer fireman, had gone through the house and told Ann not to go in because of gas."

They eventually connected, found their children all safe and counted their blessings. They lost some cattle but not as many as others had.

Although the windows blew in, which soaked the inside, and the back end suffered some damage, the house was otherwise intact. "The reason the house stood was because the barn and the other outbuildings took the wind, and the wind was deflected from the house," Gary said. "So the house really didn't move. It cracked everything, but we couldn't have afforded to do a new house because we had just bought the farm. So we decided to live with that we had. I think we were happy we made the right decision."

Like he said earlier, hindsight has clear vision. "It's just amazing how I've been so lucky," Gary said. "I don't know if I made this point, but when you hear a storm is coming, a car is not the best place to be. It's the worst place in the world. And I was blessed by the fact that a utility pole…maybe ten inches…was there. If that pole hadn't been there, why, I'd have kept going."

Help Comes from Many Sources

Gary's cousin and Lloyd's son, Jim Turner, had gone into town that day. Jim was on his way to Kirkland but detoured to DeWane's because of the foul weather.

"While I was in there, a veterinarian who was from [Kansas] hollered over the PA, 'Everybody take shelter. There's a tornado coming,'" Jim said. "I looked out the front window of that sale barn, and I saw a home that was on the top of the hill on Genoa Road blow up. And I knew we were in big trouble."

Jim sought shelter in the area under the cement bleachers. "Soon, all of the people came down from the crowd and were piled all over me," he said. "There was about thirty seconds when the tornado hit that I thought I was going to die.

"The vacuum was so great that nobody could breathe. That only lasted for a short time, and then we all took a deep breath at the same time."

Because of its steel roof, the building itself survived, and so did its dozens of occupants. "We were all cut up with a little glass and dirt, but there was nothing very severe," Jim said. "I walked outside, and cars and trucks were strewn all over, and people were in various states of emergencies. My truck was gone."

Jim left the building soon enough to see the tornado continue its tear through Boone County. "It was headed directly for our farm," he said. "I looked across that field and I could follow the back of that tornado. I watched it go across the field.

"I knew it was headed right for our farm, and my folks were home."

Jim saw that his truck was gone, so he flagged down a car and jumped into the front seat.

"They were well-to-do people from the city, from the Chicago area," he said. "We got to the top of the hill [on Logan Avenue or U.S. 20], where the Lanning farm was, and there was a tree in the way. I jumped out to help move those trees, and the guy drove off and left me. Well, it was only a matter of minutes until another man came along and said, 'Can I help anybody?' I said, 'You can give me a ride home.'"

The Good Samaritan drove Jim down U.S. 20 to Epworth Road and then north to Lawrenceville Road.

"We turned west toward our farm, and I noticed that the two farms at the top of the hill—the Pfluger farm and the Henninger farm—all of the buildings were gone," Jim said. "It wasn't much fun going over the top of the hill."

That's because he was stunned by what he saw.

"My home was completely ripped off its foundation and carried about forty or fifty yards," he said. "My parents' home was a two-story structure, [and] the top half was gone. All of our farm buildings were flat. We had dead animals lying around the yard."

He found his mother in the yard, and she told him that his father had taken his injured cousin Gary to the hospital.

Jim tried to help others sort out the disaster. "It was just the chaos.... Everybody was kind of running around in circles," he said.

One set of neighbors, a woman and two children, was found in the basement of their house. West of his farm, another farm lost seven buildings. Another neighbor lost a full herd of cows when the barn collapsed on them.

"We had a basement barn, an old stone wall about seven feet high," he said. "It took the top of the barn off and carried it, but the cattle that were inside the barn were perfect. They were just sitting there, eating hay."

Jim's wife had taken their three youngest daughters to choir practice and dropped the youngest at a friend's house. While they were accounted for, their oldest daughter, Teri, wasn't. They knew she would have been on a school bus about the time the tornado struck. So they went to look for her.

"My wife and I tried to go to the schoolhouse a couple of times, [but] the cops stopped us," he said. "Then, we would try a different direction, then we lost our car." Sharp debris on roads punctured car tires, rendering the vehicles useless. "We left two cars, just walked away from them," said Jim. But, he said, "that was the least of our worries. We were hunting for our little girl."

Eventually, a man who had good luck driving that day being able to avoid the debris and broken glass that were causing flat tires for so many others got them into town. The couple went to Jim's brother-in-law's Roy Smiley's house to regroup and get dry clothes. They were still looking for Teri, and they knew that some of the riders on her bus had been killed.

They searched the Community Building for Teri—no luck. About 8:00 p.m., they planned to drive to Rockford to hunt for her at the city's hospitals. "Some people were going to the morgue, and we weren't interested in that," Jim said.

But before they left, a friend, Dick Thomas, pulled up in front of the house. "He said he had [our] little girl," Jim said. Dick had been at Belvidere High School, where he found Teri waiting in the library. He took her to his house and eventually brought her home, to the relief of her parents.

The next day about 6:00 a.m., Jim was sitting on a bale of hay in his yard, crying over what he had lost.

"My dad came along and said, 'You know. Are you going to sit on that bale of hay all day or are you going to get up and get going?'" Jim said. "He said, 'We're going to go to several wakes and funerals in the next week, and we don't have to sponsor any of them.'

"I said, 'You're right.'"

That Monday night, Jim borrowed a pair of pants and went to his first meeting as a member of the school board.

Amazingly, Jim's house survived the tornado relatively intact—even though it had been picked up and dropped near an apple orchard. It lost its ceiling, but the framing survived. "It was all nailed together with a tongue-in-groove lumber" called shiplap, which was common at the time, Jim said.

"My wife had a loaf of bread sitting on the top of the refrigerator to rise. Like I said, the house moved forty or fifty yards, and the roof was gone and was leaning up against these trees. Well, there on the top of the refrigerator sat that damn loaf of bread."

The Turners eventually built a new home, with a bedroom for each of their four daughters.

"We kind of landed on our feet," Jim said.

But the Turners and others had a lot of help along the way.

Chapter 9

EXTRAORDINARY SURVIVAL STORIES

Even fifty years later, some tornado survivors can vividly recall their experiences, down to the smallest detail. What happened to them that day will never be forgotten, and many still carry physical and emotional scars. Three such stories that began on the most routine of days had twists of fate that are profound to this day.

Diane Shattuck and her twin sister, Debbie, were ten-year-old students at Immanuel Lutheran School on April 21, 1967. They were on the third or fourth bus in line at the high school when the bus driver alerted them of the tornado and told them to run to safety. They didn't get far. "When [the driver] opened the door, the wind just sucked us out," Diane said. Their books, Bibles and possessions went flying as they smacked into the bus in front of them. As they tried to run to the school, the tornado caught them, even though they tried to hold hands. "I went one way; she went one way," Diane said. "Then we rolled. I remember rolling over people. It didn't actually pick me up. I got hit in the mouth with a brick. My teeth were loose. My teeth are all fake now in the front. I got hit in the back of the head, too."

When they finally got to the school, Diane, who had been fully dressed with shoes, socks, a skirt, blouse and a coat, wore only her training bra and underwear. "It took everything off," she said. As she ran toward the school, she found her sister. Both were covered in mud. The girls first went to the gym and were told to go to the library. "We walked through the halls, which were [covered in glass], and we were barefoot," she said. "Someone gave us sweat clothes to put on because we were cold." They sat with their heads against the wall. When Diane got up, Debbie noticed blood dripping down the wall. "Sure enough, our heads were split open from ear to ear," Diane said.

And so they sat, waiting for help, hoping to see their parents. "People were walking by, trying to find their families," she said. "Debbie and I wondered, 'Who's going to find us?'" They lived in Caledonia with grandparents and knew their mother had gone shopping in Rockford. Their father was a truck driver in Chicago. "There was no way to make calls," she said. "All lines were down."

And still they sat. "We sat there forever. You'd think somebody would go by and know you," Diane said. She believes it was eight o'clock when one of the high school art teachers saw them and said, "You've been sitting here long enough. You're going to the hospital." Diane knew she was hurt because when she tried to rise, she couldn't. She found out later that a piece of wood had pierced her knee. She eventually lost her kneecap. The art teacher took them to Rockford's St. Anthony Hospital, which they were told was full. So they went to Swedish-American Hospital. The art teacher carried the girls to his car, Diane recalled. "I remember he had these pink Pepto-Bismol things in his glove compartment. He said, 'Do you want one?' We said yes. We were so hungry and thirsty, but we were still swallowing dirt."

At Swedish-American, staff members worked at scrubbing the mud off the two girls. "They took buckets of water and brushes that were really bristly—you know, the ones they wash floors with? That's what they used to wash us," she said. "That was painful. We were black, blue, yellow and purple for two weeks. We kept telling them that we had long blonde hair, and they didn't believe us. They didn't wash our hair because of possible [head] injuries."

Hearing of the storm, their mother went to Belvidere to look for them. Because the girls were still by themselves, radio stations broadcast their names and where they were. "Somehow, our father heard our names on the radio," Diane said. At one point, Diane noticed a man next to her whom she recognized as her father's co-worker. "He said, 'Don't worry. Everybody knows where you are at. They're coming for you. They'll be here soon.'" Diane said their parents looked in every room at the hospital until they found the girls. Diane had a badly damaged knee; a board had smacked Debbie in the back, taking out a piece of her lower back. Both had head lacerations.

Because the girls hadn't been allowed to wash their hair, when they woke up in the hospital the next morning, they were lying in "grass, mud, anything that was in our hair," Diane said. "We couldn't wash our hair for a week.

Finally, when we got to wash our hair, they said, 'You're right. You have blonde hair.'" In addition to the head injuries, the sisters had cuts from head to toe. "There wasn't one part of our bodies that wasn't cut," Diane said. "The sheets were so rough and scratchy, so they brought us sheep[skin] rugs, and oh, they were so soft."

Their stay was extended when each developed a staph infection. "We were in the hospital for a couple of months," she said. "We had to go into isolation for a while, just when we were getting ready to go home." Diane believes they were the last tornado victims to leave Swedish-American. "We didn't see anyone else," she said.

When Diane was about to be released, her knee swelled up, and when she removed the bandage, she found a piece of wood. Even fifty years later, reminders of the tornado literally come to the surface. "I get little pockets, and then there will be glass," she said. In 1971, she had so many recurring knee problems that it was replaced. She has had dental problems as well. (Debbie didn't have continuing health issues due to her injuries sustained in the tornado, but she died of cancer.)

Through all of it, Diane said she was never knocked out. "I remember getting hit in the head and seeing stars. They told my mom, 'Thank God for the mud because it stopped the bleeding.' We were lucky," she said. "Pretty lucky."

Beth (Dulgar) Funnsinn, a member of the Belvidere High School class of 1967, was on the first bus by the gym behind the school. As she started to get off the bus, the tornado struck. Badly injured, she was taken to St. Joseph's Hospital, placed on a gurney that was wheeled under a set of cupboards and literally left for dead. "A priest and a nun came in to give me the last rites," she said. The priest noticed her move and said, "She's alive!"

Doctors quickly operated on her and repaired a ruptured liver and collapsed lung. "I had mud and debris in my mouth and throat," she said. "I had lost a lot of blood." However, she recovered, and years later, when she had a C-section, something unusual occurred. "The anesthesiologist recognized the scar on my stomach," she said. "He came into my room [later] and asked how I got it. I told him about the tornado. He replied, 'I was the one who operated on you that day!'"

A Dream Dashed

Things were going well for Barbara Ann Kaiser in the spring of 1967. She was about to graduate from Belvidere High School and, for the first time, complete a full academic year at one school. April 21 already was memorable because she had picked up the white box wrapped in a blue ribbon that contained her graduation announcements and the class ring she had ordered earlier in the school year. In addition, she was a nurse's aide at St. Joseph's Hospital, and later that Friday, she was scheduled to take her nurse's entrance exam. As she left school, wearing new clothes and white shoes and carrying a new purse, she recalled that "it started out to be a beautiful spring day. My dream of being a nurse was almost ready to begin. That dream was shattered just a few minutes later."

When she left school about 3:50 p.m., she noticed the sky was dark and threatening rain. "Suddenly, it started to rain and huge hail was pounding my head," she said. Barbara ran to Martha Wyman's 1957 Chevy and jumped in the back, joining Ralph Gorham, Bonnie Smith and her sister Mary Kaiser. "Almost immediately, the contents of the large school air conditioner poured into our car, covering us with tar or coal." Then the car windows broke and the vehicle and occupants were lifted into the air by the tornado. "[It] tossed us like a toothpick over the tops of other cars in the parking lot, into an area close to the football field," she said. The car turned over several times, she recalled, as they saw buses, other cars, animals, people—"including children"—tossed in the air. "I saw the tops of telephone poles," she said. "One large truck came very close to our car, and I remember reaching out to push it out of the way. I was being twisted and turned, as were the other students in the car. I did not scream as it seemed I was not afraid, maybe because it happened so fast."

Barbara was on the right side of the back seat when the car hit the ground on its roof and then flipped over its front and landed right side up. "I was under the front seat, folded backward, and the seat and students [were] on top of me," she said. She had placed her feet under the front seat before the storm hit. "When I started to get out, not realizing I was injured, there was a piece of metal through my knee, and it anchored me to the floor," she said. She saw a two-by-four in the car, and attached to it was a chunk of her hair. Her sister was wedged in the trunk, only a hand visible. "She bit her tongue and was bleeding," Barbara said. "By then, we were all pretty much in shock. Everything seemed to be going in slow motion. I didn't feel any pain."

All five students in the car survived the harrowing ride. The others helped Barbara get out, freeing her knee from the jagged metal. Supporting one another, they staggered to the gym. "There were cars, buses, bleeding people and debris everywhere," she said. "And blood—so much blood and crying." In the gym, Barbara remembered her sister Mary saying, "Will someone who is calmer than I am please help my sister?" Barbara's knee was badly gashed, so a boy took cording out of his windbreaker and tied it around her knee. "Someone tried to get me to lie down on the floor, but I seemingly could not move," she said. "Peggy Trueblood, LPN, was there and asked several boys to help me to the floor. Peggy put one finger on my forehead and gave a little push, and the boys gently took me to the floor." While lying prone, she didn't realize how badly injured she was, so she started telling other students to get towels, anything that would stop bleeding, from the locker rooms. "You see," she said, "I was always a nurse. Even then I was trying to do first aid."

Soon, the injured were taken from the gym. "There were students lying everywhere. Adults and students were carrying the injured into the gym, and some of them were put over against the wall," she said. "I learned later those students and adults did not make it. The rescue and triage started to take place. Every drivable car and any other form of transportation were used to take the injured to the hospitals. My dad used his station wagon to take several students home or to the hospital."

Barbara was put on a classroom door and carried to a hearse. "I even joked and said this was an unusual way to go to the hospital," she said. "I was soaked and started shaking with cold and probably shock. Mr. Jason Jury Sr. found a blanket and covered me. He helped put me in the hearse."

But she wasn't alone. "As I was lying there, a child was also put into the hearse," she said. "I took [his] hand and held it all the way to the hospital. The little one was whimpering and calling for mommy. The child seemed to have severe leg injuries, and there was so much blood. On the way to St. Joseph's Hospital, the little hand went limp and the whimpering stopped. When we got to the hospital, I heard them say not to bring the child [in because the child] did not make it. I never knew the name of that child, and it has never left me when the little hand went limp. Someday I hope to find out the name of this precious little one. I have always thought it was a boy but because of the mud and injuries do not know for sure."

When she got to St. Joseph's, she saw her co-workers busy in the emergency room. "I was pretty upset that I could not get up and help," she said. "[They] didn't recognize me. I was put on the examining table, and a veterinarian immediately started to work on my cuts. He stitched up the gash on my knee and did not use any deadening medication, as I still did not feel any pain. Then a couple of nuns lifted me onto a treatment table and pushed me into another waiting area. As I was lying there, people kept coming in to find their children."

Barbara was in a long line of gurneys awaiting an X-ray when she saw her mother slowly walking up the hallway, looking at every face. "She and Dad had been looking for my sister and me throughout the afternoon. Mary was at St. Anthony Hospital. They even checked the morgue, as I was not on any list of students who had been brought in. Mom walked right past me and didn't know it was me. I very weakly called her name several times, but there was a lot of dirt and tar from the air conditioner, so I could hardly whisper. She finally heard me and came running over to the cart. We cried together. My mom's tears were so precious. She had been told by a boy running past our house that a tornado had hit the school and everyone was dead."

X-rays revealed that Barbara had several fractures in her lower back, neck and skull, as well as sinus fractures, several broken ribs, displaced kneecaps and fractures in her feet and thumb. In addition, she had a great deal of embedded dirt and glass. Later, it was found she had ruptured eardrums, internal injuries and dislocated hips. The employee of St. Joseph's became a patient.

Thus the rehabilitation began, which continues to this day. Told she would never walk, she said, "I [said] I was going to be a nurse, and a nurse cannot work in a wheelchair." With the aid of a therapist named Sam, she was lifted into the whirlpool tub daily. "I finished my senior year in that whirlpool!" she said.

Barbara left the hospital on June 8, 1967, the day before commencement, "so that I could participate in the program. The procession line looked like a group of injured soldiers coming home," she said. "There were people in wheelchairs, on crutches and some empty chairs on the platform."

Her dream of being a nurse had to be put on hold. She had five years of therapy and forty-four surgeries to repair broken bones, her spine, eardrums, sinuses and ears. "To this day, I struggle with constant pain in many of the areas," she said. "I have no hearing in one ear. I have knee replacements."

In time, she was able to start her training as a nurse and become an LPN. She was able to work three years at Rockford Memorial Hospital "and loved every minute of my time there," she said. "I worked in as many areas as possible, as I knew my time as a nurse would be short-lived. There was too much pain. I could not even lift a premature infant."

Barbara then went into education, teaching third grade for twenty years. "But due to pain and limited motion, [I] had to retire from Silver State Baptist School in Colorado." She works in a sit-down job as a medical transcriptionist in Denver, but "the pain never stops.

"My memories of that day have never dimmed," she said. She thinks about the child whose hand she held in the hearse; how so many helped her, including Mr. Jury and the medical staff; about the parents who looked for their children and found them in the morgue. "Even a funny thought: 'Where did all of my new clothes and class ring go?' My bankbook was returned to me. It was found near Beloit, Wisconsin. The class ring that I cherished at that time was never found or replaced.

"But all in all, I am very thankful that the Lord kept my family and so many other families in His hand. He has helped me throughout my life to endure the pain and to be as calm as possible whenever there is a storm. My thoughts go out to all the families involved in this horrible tornado. It still brings tears to think about it, even after forty-nine years."

Chapter 10

LIFE-CHANGING DECISIONS

Split-second decisions made at crucial moments on a disastrous day by many people all over Belvidere saved many lives. The details of these stories are still remembered.

It had been a good year for Donald Fisher. In June 1966, he got a job at the Chrysler Assembly Plant, and within a year, he had a home built for his family on the corner of West Tenth Street and Maple Avenue. He was home with his wife and three young children that April afternoon when he happened to look out his bay window. "I saw the cloud on the ground, coming our way from the southwest—that's where a tornado always comes from," he said. "All I could do was holler, 'Tornado!'

"I grabbed my three kids and [knew] that we all had to get to the basement. I was dragging the youngest one, Carla, who was a year old, by her arm. I knew I had only split seconds to go, but I dragged them all down [to] the basement." Donald wrapped his arms around his wife and children and scrambled down the basement steps. "I think I had my foot on the bottom step of the stairway," he said. "The next thing I knew, my daughter was starting to cry. She said, 'Daddy? Daddy? Where's our house?' When I looked up, I saw the sky. All we had left was the hole in the ground. My wife remembers the noise. She said it sounded like a big ole freight train. I don't remember the noise. All I had on my mind was the kids and her."

All were uninjured except the family dog. The part German Shepherd, part Collie was in the basement too but suffered a broken leg, which had to be amputated. However, she was able to walk on three legs. While working his full-time job at Chrysler, Donald rebuilt their home. The family lived in the basement of a home outside the city while he put up the house. It was still the family residence in 2016. "To this day, if there's a warning or a watch, I still go to my bay window, just to see," he said.

There was one more side note to the family's story. Among the many household items lost was Donald's son Douglas Eugene Fisher's birth certificate. A few weeks later, it was found seventy miles away in a cornfield near Union Grove, Wisconsin.

On sale days, Howard Ardenfeld routinely parked his car sideways in front of DeWane's Restaurant and Auction Barn. Ardenfeld was a cattle buyer for Oscar Mayer, then and now a famous maker of meat products. When the dozens of people at DeWane's heard of the impending storm, Ardenfeld began to run out the front door through the restaurant at the front of the building to his car. "My sister, Jean Farina, was at the door," Ray DeWane said, "and Howard was going to run out and get into his car. Well, my sister said, 'No. You're not going. Get over here and get behind the counter.'" After the storm passed, Howard went to his car and found that a two-by-four had been driven through the driver's side. Jean's decision helped save his life. "He'd have been dead," Ray said.

Karen Cross can't remember the name of the man who drove her bus that day, but she is convinced he saved lives, including possibly hers. He drove the first bus to leave BHS after school because he had two afternoon routes. Karen was running late and, with an eye on the darkening sky, wanted to get home. As she hurried, the stubborn lock on her locker stuck, but she was able to get it open, snatch her jacket and run out the door to the bus, which was leaving. "I knocked on the door just as he started to take off," she said. "I pounded on the door, asking if he would let me in."

He did, and bus No. 12 went north on East Avenue. Just before the turn at Logan Avenue, the riders noticed two police squad cars screaming toward the high school. The second of the two stopped, and the officer motioned for the driver to turn the bus around, indicating the driver should return the bus to the high school. "I don't know why, but the driver shook his head no," Karen said. "We were [near] the high school, but he just kept going. We got on Logan and got to Penney's [now Alpine Bank] when one of the kids in the back was looking down [South] State Street and hollered, 'Oh my God, there's a tornado!'

"I swear, this bus driver took off and drove ninety miles an hour down [North] State Street....He went so fast. When we got to the north side, it started to hail." The driver stopped the bus and told the students to duck under the seats while hail pummeled the vehicle. When the hail stopped, he drove them to Perry School, where all of the teachers were standing outside. "[The teachers] came running to us and said, 'Didn't you know a tornado hit the high school?'" The students unloaded and went into the school for safety's sake. Karen's mother heard the news and "prayed that I was on the bus," Karen said. "I was...but I almost missed it.

"I wish I could remember [the bus driver's] name. Was it a life-changing decision? Yes. If we had turned around, we'd probably have been in the worst of it...and I might not be here."

Karen has another vivid memory of that day. She was sitting in the front seat when she saw the two squad cars drive up East Avenue toward the high school. "These cars were going fast, but I think Dutch Whalen was in the first one," she said.

Whalen, the police captain, is considered one of the heroes of that afternoon. Many recall seeing him drive down East Avenue, responding to a radio report of a tornado headed toward the high school. Whalen had his siren blaring as he waved and yelled at students to get to safety. Karen likely witnessed him speeding to the school, where his warnings saved lives.

Chapter 11

A RESCUE OF IMMENSE PROPORTIONS

Norma Duclon had just gotten home from a busy and hectic day at her job in the surgical room of St. Joseph's Hospital in Belvidere when she received an emergency call to return. She was summoned because "a tornado had hit Belvidere and injured people were being brought into the emergency room," she said, recalling a plea on radio and TV asking for doctors, nurses and other medical professionals to come to Belvidere and help.

"When I arrived at the hospital, the scene I gazed upon was horrible," she said. "The lobby was lined with the injured children and incoherent and sobbing parents. As I made my way to the emergency room, I saw that every available cart and stretcher was occupied by a child covered with mud and blood.

"Aides and nurses were busy with pails of water and rags, washing the mud from these young children so doctors could find the injuries and treat them. Immediate lifesaving care was given to those who needed it, and the less injured were asked to sit on the floor in the waiting room to await their turn to be examined."

Some of the victims sat quietly, probably in shock from the disaster or loss of blood and fluids; others screamed hysterically; and others calmly described the destruction wrought by the tornado.

One crying boy told Norma that Belvidere High School had been directly in the tornado's path and that most of the school buses there were hit or damaged. These buses, he said, carried children ready to be taken

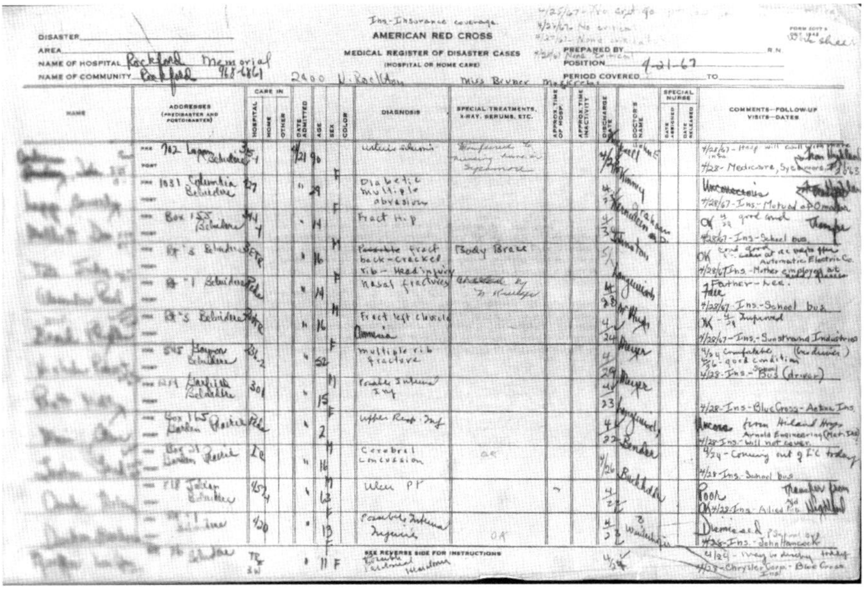

AMERICAN RED CROSS
MEDICAL REGISTER OF DISASTER CASES
(HOSPITAL OR HOME CARE)

DISASTER
AREA
NAME OF HOSPITAL Rockford Memorial
NAME OF COMMUNITY
PREPARED BY
POSITION
PERIOD COVERED 4-21-67 TO

NAME	ADDRESSES (PREDISASTER AND POSTDISASTER)	CARE IN: HOSPITAL	HOME	OTHER	DATE ADMITTED	AGE	SEX	COLOR	DIAGNOSIS	SPECIAL TREATMENTS, X-RAY, SERUMS, ETC.	APPROX. TIME OF HOSP.	APPROX. TIME INACTIVITY	DISCHARGE DATE	DOCTOR'S NAME	SPECIAL NURSE: DATE ASSIGNED	DATE RELEASED	COMMENTS—FOLLOW-UP VISITS—DATES
									Diabetic, multiple abrasion								4/28- Medicare
	Box 155 Belvidere								Fract hip								
						16	M		back - cracked rib - Head injury	Body Brace							4/28/67-Ins.-School bus
							F		nasal fracture								
						16	M		Fract left clavicle								4/28/67-Ins.-School bus
						52	F		multiple rib fracture								
						15											4/28-Ins.-Blue Cross-Aetna Ins
						16	M		Cerebral concussion								4/28-Ins.-School bus
						13											

SEE REVERSE SIDE FOR INSTRUCTIONS

The actual record of some patients who were treated on April 21, 1967, at Swedish-American Hospital. *Courtesy of Paul Greenland.*

home. Norma then came to an alarming discovery—her children had been on one of the buses.

"When I listened to the sobbing boy's story, fear began to grip my heart," she said. "My two children were on one of the buses. While comforting and helping these children, I prayed to God for my children's safety. I kept wondering if the next one brought in would be my own child and whether or not I would have the courage to face seeing my child stilled forever."

But, as a professional, she worked on and gauged the scope of the tragedy. "The storm picked up the buses," she said, "turning them over and over, smashing them to the ground. Glass flew through the air like bullets shot from a gun, and tar and wood were embedded in the skin and scalps of most of the children on the buses. The majority of the children helped that night were a mass of cuts, bruises and road gravel embedded into their body and skin."

Unfortunately, many had more severe injuries. One boy was brought in on the back of a truck and had an eight-foot board through his thigh, she recalled. "An orderly hurried to the basement to find a wood saw to cut the board off before the boy could be moved from the truck," she said. "The board was removed as delicately as possible, and I heard he had to have extensive and delicate surgery to save his life.

An injured student is in need of help at St. Joseph's Hospital. *Courtesy of Boone County Historical Museum.*

"Two of the most horrible cases were taken immediately to surgery," Norma said. The first was Linda (Trueblood) Lehman, who "had been partially scalped" and had to be sedated while waiting for an anesthesiologist to arrive from the nearest city, Rockford, before surgery could begin. "Her scalp hung loose, exposing her head, which was covered with tar and sand," Norma said. Fortunately, Linda survived; the other "horrible" case didn't.

"A boy had crushing injuries to his head, and the doctors fought in vain for one hour to keep him alive," she said. "Tears came to my eyes when I saw him being taken away to wait in the morgue for his unsuspecting parents to identify his body."

Then, a doctor came with startling news that there were at least seven dead at the high school. "I fought to keep my composure, all the while wondering if one of those was mine. My will to keep on was difficult, but I kept thinking that I would help these children and, somewhere, someone would help mine," Norma said. "My husband went through severe trauma as he was searching for our children. Each time a new body was found, he suffered until the identity was made."

Desperate Searches

Randall Trueblood experienced the same gut-wrenching experience trying to find his daughter Linda. He had already been to the high school and, in his station wagon, ferried an injured boy to St. Joe's, only to have the boy, the station wagon and its teenage driver—who did not have a driver's license—sent to Rockford Memorial Hospital. An estimated twenty to twenty-five station wagons and trucks were pressed into similar emergency use that day.

"So I stayed at the hospital," Randall said. "My mother-in-law was there, and she had picked up my wife, [and] all three of us looked and we couldn't find our daughter."

So the three headed for Highland Hospital, a few blocks from their home, and were surprised to see how much damage it had sustained. By that time, most of the seriously injured people had been sent to St. Joseph's or one of the Rockford hospitals.

In the basement of the hospital, they saw several children "all hunkered down," Randall said. "I did see one of my daughter's friends, Molly Pratt. She lived across the street from us. But Linda wasn't there."

At that point, the Trueblood group realized they had to check the hospitals in Rockford. Their first stop was St. Anthony Hospital on Rockford's far east side, which was inundated with people looking for injured relatives and friends.

Cars were parked along the entrance road and on the lawn. "I don't know how we got up to the hospital, but there were no records of her," Randall said. "So then we went to Swedish-American Hospital."

The trip farther into Rockford took longer than normal because of the crush of cars, rescue vehicles and other vehicles. "All of this took so much time because there was so much traffic," he said. "You couldn't get to a phone, and when you did find one, you had to wait in line. So we got to Swedish-American and found there was no record of her there."

Realizing that the time to drive to Rockford's west side and Rockford Memorial would be daunting, Randall found a phone and called the hospital instead. But it had no record of Linda's admission.

It would be decades before instant communication would become available in the form of cellphones and pagers. So after hearing that Randall would have to continue his search, he held the phone up and asked people standing nearby, "Does somebody want me to ask for someone at Rockford Memorial?" Randall said that somebody then asked about Barbara Johnson and took the phone from him.

Randall was quiet for a moment as he recalled this story because Johnson was one of the tornado's victims.

"I don't know if it was her parents or who asked," he said. "I'd love to know that."

Having personally checked four hospitals and called a fifth without any kind of news, Randall turned to his wife and said that they would have to make yet another stop—at a temporary morgue back in Belvidere.

They made their way back to the car, where Randall's mother was waiting for them. Just as Randall was telling his wife about the morgue, his mother said, "Hurry! Hurry! Hurry! I just heard your name over the radio. You're wanted at St. Joseph's Hospital."

So they hurried back to Belvidere and St. Joseph's, where Linda had been all along but unidentified. When they got there, Barbara Kaiser, a BHS senior who was being treated for her serious injuries, recognized them. "Mr. and Mrs. Trueblood came in, and I told them that Linda was on the table across from me," Barbara said. "She was horribly injured from a head injury and was unconscious. No one recognized her, and I was able to tell them who she was."

Linda's survival story is one of the most dramatic of the day. She had been in Circle Drive in a neighbor's car when the tornado struck. She was one of three girls sitting in the back seat of the car and, seemingly, had weathered the storm. Then the car was pulled into the air.

"Linda was sucked out of the car," her father said. "She was the only one missing from the car."

Linda, who cannot recall a single event of the day, said others told her what happened. "All I know is that the driver of the car, a neighbor, told us girls to lock our arms," she said. "There were three of us in the back, two in the front. I was in the middle of the back seat, and the car went up about fifty feet, then I flew out of the window about seventy-five feet up."

The neighbor found her lying facedown in the mud. "He turned her over and saw he could not attend to her," Randall said. "How she got to the hospital, she doesn't know. She was almost scalped."

"The only part of the story I know is what people tell me," she said. "As a mother with a son, I can imagine how frantic I would be…to think what they went through, looking for me, and especially finding me in the shape I was in."

A Nurse's Dilemma

Norma, who shared the experience with the Truebloods and dozens of others, continued to work at St. Joseph's while her husband searched for their children. Several hours later—which Norma said seemed like "an eternity"—her husband was able to let her know that her son was at home and her daughter was in a Rockford hospital.

"I thanked God and continued to work the rest of the night and the next day doing what I could to help the less fortunate," she said. Her daughter's bus had flipped over twice, and she had been knocked unconscious. "She lay on the inside roof of the bus, where a large boulder had crashed through the bottom of the bus and landed next to her head," Norma said.

The May 7, 1967 edition of the *Belvidere Daily Republican* reported that St. Joseph's Hospital was overwhelmed with injured survivors that Friday. When the tornado struck, sixty-two of the hospital's one hundred beds were occupied. In a matter of hours, 40 more patients were admitted and at least 125 were treated and released. Doctors, dentists and nurses from around the area rushed to Belvidere to help out at St. Joseph's.

Many of those came from Highland Hospital, which was forced to close at 9:30 p.m. because of damage it sustained in the tornado. "The spirit of the Highland staff was great," said Sister Mary Luke of St. Joseph's. "We all tried to work together. There was such an overwhelming response from everyone. By 3:00 a.m. Saturday, things were pretty normal.

"Doctors and others worked even though they had not located their own children. One of the remarkable things was the reaction of the teenagers. They certainly proved themselves. They were absolutely remarkable." Sister Mary Luke said she saw no hysteria or overreaction, even from the students who had been severely injured.

She said it was nearly impossible to estimate how many volunteers helped in the recovery, rescue and hospital effort. "Many of them left without our knowing who they were," she said. "There are so many people that we can't reach."

Sister Mary Luke said that medical personnel came from Rockford, DeKalb and Sycamore and that five student nurses and a graduate student from Mercy Hospital in Janesville, Wisconsin, helped out on Friday, Saturday and Sunday. All of the hospital's employees and eighteen of the nuns, including four who were not nurses, worked throughout the weekend.

Winnebago County Civil Defense director Eugene O'Malley said that at least 350 people were treated in area hospitals.

One of those was Belvidere fire chief Jim Lantz, who survived being picked up by the tornado three times but needed medical attention. He was taken to St. Joseph's Hospital, where he was X-rayed and told to sit on a cot and not move.

Then a doctor came by whom Jim knew. "I told him what had happened, how badly I was hurt," Jim said. "He said he would find out what he could." The doctor checked Jim's X-rays and found that while he had no broken bones, he had two vertebrae out of place.

"[The doctor] said I think you'd better stay tonight, and I said, 'Doc, I've got a lot of things to do in the morning,'" Jim said. "He said, 'I don't think you're going to do much in the morning,' and he was right. I couldn't get out of bed for two days."

Jim then returned to work to help supervise the removal of drugs from Highland Hospital. A couple days later, he learned he had suffered a concussion. "That kind of slowed me for a while, too," he said. "But I had a lot of good men working for me at the time."

Sadly, a firefighter's wife was killed and an ex-firefighter's son lost his life at the high school.

The *Chicago Tribune* reported on Sunday, April 23, that Ralph Morgan, coordinator of civil defense for northern Illinois, ran field operations from the Boone County sheriff's office.

"First we coordinated rescue work, which went on through the night," Ralph told the *Tribune*. "We were handicapped by darkness. This morning, the National Guard is conducting a search of open fields for victims and civil air patrol volunteers and others are lifting up the debris where houses stood to search for other victims."

Some minor cases of looting were reported, but Mayor Hetland said that no arrests were made.

The *Chicago Tribune* also reported that more than one thousand victims and volunteer workers had been fed at the Community Building. Grace

Fossati, regional director for the Red Cross disaster service for the central states, said that seven mobile canteens had been set up from Milwaukee, St. Louis, Des Moines and Michigan. About thirty people stayed at the emergency shelter that had been set up. Most of those who had homes damaged or destroyed stayed with friends or relatives or simply made do. "The victims prefer to remain with their homes, picking up what they can," Fossati said. By 8:00 p.m. on the night of the tornado, the Red Cross unit from Rockford had registered about two hundred people.

The Salvation Army set up three canteens at the disaster scene from which food was distributed.

Hospitals Cope with a Disaster

St. Anthony Hospital in Rockford used its "disaster plan" to cope with the crush of injured persons. According to the *Rockford Morning Star*, doctors said the biggest problem was "determining where the injuries were under the mud, dirt and blood."

The *Rockford Register Star* in 1995 reported that the hospital's signal to start the disaster plan was "Code Black." As a result, volunteers poured in. Retired nurses returned to work; doctors came from Madison, Wisconsin, and Chicago.

Three hospital employees left a bowling alley in the middle of a game to come and help. The parking lot and driveways were so jammed that emergency vehicles drove across the lawn to get to the cafeteria, where patients were being admitted.

More than fifty injured survivors waited for treatment at one time—most of them children.

In a 1991 newsletter describing the hospital's response to the disaster, Kathleen Mangiaracina, the nurse who was the director of the operating room, said, "We took the most severely injured first, the ones with ruptured kidneys and chest wounds. We saw one boy none of us will ever forget; he had a two-by-four stuck through his thigh. We treated abdominal and spleen injuries, huge lacerations, broken bones, large gouges, head injuries, the usual type of trauma."

The operating room crew worked until four o'clock the next morning.

Nursing shift supervisor Bernie Kudzma said the hospital's patient-filled cafeteria "looked like a battlefield." The hospital was busy for a week, with staffers working eighteen- to twenty-hour shifts.

"They didn't say, 'I have to be paid for this,'" Bernie said. "And they didn't stop when they were hungry or tired."

Geographically, Swedish-American Hospital is the second closest among Rockford hospitals to Belvidere, so it was the next place ambulances and other vehicles with injured tornado survivors headed. But vital information was not getting through because the tornado had knocked out power lines, including those between Rockford and Belvidere. Reporting in *Heartbeat*, Swedish-American's newsletter, Nurse Shirley Powell said that at 5:30 p.m., the hospital had no idea how many casualties to expect, although staffers knew school buses had been overturned. Their best source of news was from reports on transistor radios. At 5:45 p.m., Shirley and other nurses received a call to report to the hospital. "At that time, the sirens of approaching emergency vehicles could be heard," she said. As soon as the injured students arrived at the emergency entrance from Belvidere, other injured people began to appear. Several men, including hospital employees and visitors, began unloading ambulances, trucks, buses, station wagons and automobiles. The injured were carried on stretchers and doors, carried in arms or placed in wheelchairs. "We must have tagged the first fifty children within twenty minutes."

Tagging—attaching a name to a patient—was difficult, however, because many victims were in shock and some forgot their names; others were identified by schoolmates on nearby stretchers. Also, Shirley pointed out, "It was difficult to understand what some children were saying because their mouths were swollen and filled with dirt. The onrush of patients was so great that many times, [nursing] students ran alongside stretcher-bearers trying to obtain at least a name from the injured so the identity tag could be tied."

Despite the confusion, the condition of the injured and a shortage of personnel for the first twenty minutes, Shirley said that not one patient was lost to shock. In a letter to employees, Swedish-American administrator E. Dean Grout said, "About 120 patients were processed in just under 90 minutes. Everyone pitched in to help the unfortunate victims, including hospital staffers, volunteers, even ambulatory patients in a case or two, and again, it was people helping people."

Emergency surgery was performed on victims until 4:00 a.m. Saturday, and most of the hospital's medical staff remained in-house throughout the morning, Shirley said.

Eleanor O'Donnell, an LPN at Highland Hospital who survived the tornado and continued to work until told to go home, was impressed with the volunteer effort that was a result of the tornado.

"We couldn't have done it without all the volunteers who came in and helped us," Eleanor said. "We had construction workers....We had people coming in."

One of those volunteers was Ellen McHugh, an RN who heard about the tornado on the radio in her home in Rockford and decided to help.

"I threw some blankets and sheets in the car and headed to Belvidere about 5:00 p.m.," she said. She went to St. Joseph's and helped where she could. "I stayed until about 1:00 a.m., then I went back Saturday and Sunday, too."

In a story in the April 27, 1967 edition of the *Belvidere Daily Republican*, the Red Cross reported that 463 people, more than 300 of whom were schoolchildren, had been admitted to local hospitals for treatment of injuries suffered in the tornado. Of these, 277 were treated and released the same day, while 186 remained for further treatment. In all, 109 were admitted to St. Joseph's Hospital in Belvidere, 104 to St. Anthony's Hospital in Rockford, 154 to Swedish-American in Rockford and 86 to Rockford Memorial. In addition, 10 were admitted to Alma Nursing Home in Rockford. Patients at Belvidere's Highland Hospital, which was hit hard by the tornado, were sent to other places of care.

Following the tornado, the top administrators of Belvidere's two hospitals jointly issued a statement to the public:

> *The administrators and staff of St. Joseph's and Highland Hospital express their sincere appreciation to the medical staff, hospital employees, and all individuals and organizations for their spontaneous response to the disaster on Friday, April 21. Your prompt assistance evidenced your concern for other people's welfare and your desire to serve. We can only hope to thank you adequately by continuing to serve you to the very best of our ability.*

The statement was signed by Sister Mary Luke, RN, administrator, St. Joseph's Hospital, Belvidere; and Mrs. Esther Hawkey, RN, administrator, Highland Hospital.

Chapter 12

RECOVERING FROM A DISASTER

Eventually, the rescue effort was replaced by the recovery and cleanup effort, which began on Friday, hours after the tornado touched down.

John Winter was a member of the nearby Winnebago Fire Department, which answered a call for help shortly after the tornado struck. He recalled being in the area of the tornado's path in the southeast part of Belvidere. At one point that first night, he and his colleagues looked over to the tollway and Route 5 and marveled at what they saw.

"We looked on the road and saw at least one hundred vehicles in a convoy coming over the toll road, everything from dump trucks to tractors," he said. "It was like a sea of yellow lights."

The response from people from the area and region was unprecedented. The *Belvidere Daily Republican* estimated that three thousand volunteers came to Belvidere on Saturday, April 22, to help.

Many of the volunteers were skilled construction workers. The *Rockford Morning Star* reported that others came, willing to offer their "strong backs and willing hands." These people were put to work clearing trees, downed limbs and other debris from the street so other vehicles could get into the disaster areas.

Requests for specific types of equipment were made, such as trucks, chain saws, grappling rigs and portable power generators. Construction workers used equipment donated by contractors to help individual homeowners cover windows and to do some emergency patching so families could return to their homes.

In the days after the tornado, groups of volunteers, like this one, helped to clear farms and fields of debris. *Courtesy of Boone County Historical Museum.*

While the local recovery effort needed manpower, Ken Paulson, assistant civil defense director for Boone County, requested that volunteers not try to drive to the tornado-ravaged area but instead report to the courthouse, where they then would be bused into areas of need.

Sunday's *Rockford Morning Star* described a "mammoth cleanup effort [which] moved into full swing" on Saturday as men and machines "joined the fight." But before the fight could begin, the workers had to be able to get to the scene. And that prompted a warning from officials to people who merely wanted to view the destruction: stay away!

The lead paragraph of a story in Sunday's *Rockford Morning Star* read, "If you were planning on riding out to Belvidere today to take a first-hand look

Left: Snow falls on Sunday, April 23, 1967, as heavy equipment operator Eugene "Jinx" Keegan, who is helping with the cleanup effort, talks with U.S. senator Charles Percy of Illinois. *Courtesy of Boone County Historical Museum.*

Below: One of the ways to clear the overwhelming amount of debris was with fire. *Courtesy of Boone County Historical Museum.*

at the devastation caused by Friday's tornado, forget it. You won't get to see the damaged area."

A state police spokesman noted that people were trying to get through the barriers on the south side of the city, which was the worst hit. "We had a lot of trouble," said Lieutenant William Gentille.

The only people allowed into the devastated area were residents, and they got in only if they had a pass issued by officials at the Boone County Courthouse. "This is the way it's got to be run," William said. "We've got to keep people out if we ever expect to get this area cleaned up."

At that time, U.S. 20 ran through the heart of the city, down North State Street across the Kishwaukee River to the Y intersection of South State and Logan Avenue. U.S. 20 then followed Logan Avenue. Officials considered closing off the entire city, but that was unfeasible, so U.S. 20 remained open. Aside from the damage to DeWane's and other businesses on Logan Avenue, sightseers would not be able to see any of the devastation.

"Sightseers will see nothing," said Ralph Morgan, civil defense coordinator for northern Illinois. "They'll be herded right on through town."

"People who come over here for sightseeing trips will be wasting their time," added Belvidere mayor Clair Hetland. "We'll turn them back. They create a hazard and don't help us a bit."

That didn't stop people from trying, as traffic on U.S. 20 was backed up most of the day, hampering the ability of men and material to get from one part of the city to another and to the areas of greatest need.

According to the *Chicago Tribune*, caravans of public and privately owned trucks arrived to help, along with cranes, bulldozers and other pieces of heavy equipment. The *Tribune* reported, "Mayors and city officials from throughout Illinois, Indiana, Missouri, and Wisconsin phoned to volunteer aid and equipment. Auto wreckers arrived from Chicago. Generators were sent from Quincy. Telephone and electricity wiremen worked. Insurance adjusters were on the scene appraising damages and making payments."

Downed Lines and Limbs

One of the many hazards was downed power lines; Bill Hammond had one of those outside his home at 320 West Sixth Street. "There was a hot wire hanging low across the street, so Bill propped it up with a forked branch and tied a red rag on it so cars coming down the street wouldn't hit it," Barbara Hammond said. "This was a live line, and I was a wreck until he was back in the house."

She described another incident with a truck, loaded high with someone's possessions, that pulled down an electric line. The line stayed intact, so the people in the truck stopped to put up a log partially blocking the road, Barbara recalled. This ensured that other drivers would miss making contact with the wire; they'd drive under it instead. Only a few minutes later, two men with chain saws came by, thinking the road was blocked, so they sawed the log.

Other volunteers, also with chain saws, helped the Hammonds, Barbara said. "While Bill was waiting for his brother to bring his chain saw, two men, each with a chain saw, got our trees cut up, and we got most of it hauled to the street."

Clearing roads clogged by downed limbs and trees was vital to allow crews to get to the devastated areas.

John Winter, the fireman from Winnebago, was directing traffic at an intersection on the south side of town when men from a tree service came up. "They wanted to clear a road that was full of downed trees," John said. "I watched them go to this one street, and it was amazing to see. There must have been guys with six or seven chain saws, and all of a sudden, the road was open. Of course, they were all professionals. It's not like me out there with my chain saw."

John said one of the biggest problems early in the immediate cleanup phase was tires flattened by glass and other debris. "So tire repair services were out there," he said. "Rockford Blacktop sent some equipment out just to help with tires.

"Also, you never think about gas lines being broken. Now we [emergency vehicles] have plugs as standard equipment for plugging gas lines."

He was directing traffic in front of Highland Hospital when a semi-trailer drove slowly up South State Street.

"It had a big crane on a flatbed," John said. "It must have come right from a construction site. There was a guy up in the crane, and he had to swing the boom around to get through the street. He had to maneuver around everything. They were going to the high school."

Several Boy Scout troops helped, in addition to a Sea Scout group from Dixon and a group of Civil Air Patrol cadets. Boys fifteen and older were told they could come and help if they arrived in groups with an adult supervisor.

Others helped where they could. Bill Hammond and his son Doug volunteered as "runners" for the Salvation Army, Barbara Hammond said. "They were keeping the state patrolmen and National Guard supplied with coffee and sandwiches, besides supplying food, clothing and essentials to the needy families."

At the end of the month, civil defense authorities estimated that about 4,500 volunteers came to Belvidere to help.

"Everyone has been so unbelievably wonderful to us," Mayor Clair Hetland said.

"We Did What Was Needed"

On the day after the tornado, survivor Marty Prather realized how fortunate he was to have survived unscathed. So he and some friends returned to the disaster scene to help others pick up the pieces of their lives.

"I guess it was about eight o'clock [on Friday night] when everybody in our family was home, or we knew where they were," Marty said. "It was like, OK, the next day we'll go back there and help. When your family is not hurt and your house is not hurt, then you go up there to find out what you can do. Whether it is to clean up or look for stuff."

There was a lot of that going on. Mrs. Rodney Swanson, a mother of six whose home on Garfield Avenue was untouched, came to the Community Building to help at 6:00 p.m. on Friday. At 2:00 p.m. the next day, she was still there. She told the *Rockford Morning Star*, "I felt mine were safe at home in bed and other people's weren't."

Mrs. Harry Dannenberg of Rockford rushed to Swedish-American Hospital on Friday to see if she could help. Dannenberg, seventy, was a

A boy hammers a notice about Red Cross disaster services available to devastated neighborhoods in the tornado's path. *Courtesy of Boone County Historical Museum.*

retired nurse and hadn't worn her white nursing shoes in fourteen years. "We all jumped in and did what was needed," she said.

About ten Rockford College students helped to sort canned goods. Two state highway workers, Maynard Schmidt and Bernard Edwards, and their foreman, Don Pulliam, were on the scene minutes after the disaster and helped clear a way to the storm-ravaged Highland Hospital.

The hospital also was the focus of "Operation Bulldozer," organized by the Associated General Contractors of America, which arranged for end-loaders, bulldozers, cranes, utility tractors and dump trucks to help as well. Machinery came from as far away as Chicago, but among the local and area businesses that helped were Gregory Anderson, Rockford Blacktop, Charles Ind Co., Einer Nelson Construction, Belvidere Construction Co. and Shappert Engineering Co.

So much food and clothing had been offered to survivors that the Red Cross announced on Saturday night that such donations should be stopped.

Illinois governor Otto Kerner made an air and ground inspection of the devastated area and said he would ask the Illinois General Assembly to make emergency funds available. By Saturday, the U.S. Small Business Administration had declared Boone County a disaster area.

One of the most amazing recoveries took place northeast of Belvidere, where the tornado finally left Boone County before moving northeast to McHenry County and beyond. The clean, wide fields that seem to stretch to the sky as you drive along Lawrenceville to Garden Prairie Roads don't tell the story of how so many volunteers helped for so long to bring things back to order. An estimated two thousand acres of land were covered with debris, and until this debris was removed, farmers could not plant their crops.

Beginning the next day, Saturday, April 22, volunteers began to show up to ask where they could help clean the littered fields. The fields were strewn with not only the shattered remnants of everyday objects but also scores of cans, the result of the tornado smashing into a junkyard on Lawrenceville Road.

"There were just thousands and thousands of those cans," said Gary Turner, who still lives in his home on Lawrenceville Road. "And they just blew all over."

But then people came to help. "The volunteers came and picked up the fields so we could farm that year," Gary said. "It was unbelievable."

There were Boy Scouts, Mennonites from central Illinois and Belvidere High School students who knew that help was needed.

Jim Turner told the *Belvidere Daily Republican* that about two hundred men had come to help clean up his farm and fields. Jim said that trucks from the

DeKalb Highway Department and the township helped to carry out debris. And, he added, volunteers who were considering a trip to the area should come out because they would be fed with donated milk and food.

The Colonial Bakery in Rockford donated bread and other items, and most of it ended up being served by Gary and Ann Turner. Their house survived, aside from some minor damage, which meant that their kitchen was working. "We never lost our telephone, and we had a gas stove," Gary said. "So we were able to feed people. We fed people, the volunteers and other farm people. There were all kinds of people who came and helped us. We could sleep in our house—it wasn't damaged that badly—but other houses in the neighborhood were completely blown away."

Gary also noted that the Cordray brothers helped a lot by bringing their bulldozers and other heavy equipment. "They bulldozed a lot of dead animals," he said.

Within hours of the tornado, truckloads of debris had been hauled to the gravel pit on Appleton Road. Among items dumped there were the remains of roofs and walls, trees and limbs, fences, scraps of wood, paper, cloth and trash.

One of the volunteers who simply showed up at Roger Miller's farm on Lawrenceville Road was Lowell Eby, a farmer from Osceola, Indiana. He had heard radio reports of the storm damage in Belvidere and drove his pickup truck approximately 180 miles to Boone County. Eby told the *Belvidere Daily Republican* that after his farm suffered heavy damage on a Palm Sunday in 1963, several Amish came from Pennsylvania the next week and remained until the rebuilding was under control.

Returning to Normal

The *Belvidere Daily Republican* reported in the April 22, 1967 edition that all three Belvidere banks had established emergency relief funds for residents. Interest-free loans were to be paid on the basis of personal need.

Also, the Small Business Administration announced it would have representatives in Belvidere the week following the tornado to make funds available for businesses and homeowners for losses not covered by insurance.

As time went on, there were indications that things were returning to normal. Eventually, electric and phone service was restored. The city water was tested and declared safe. And tax bills went out on time.

A regular column in the *Belvidere Daily Republican* (Down on the Farm by Elder Farmer) focused on Boone County farmers on May 3, 1967:

> *The farmer has problems, far greater this year than in the past, if he happens to be one of the victims of the tragic havoc that hit us just a week ago.*
>
> *Somehow those who till the land have always seemed to measure up to their responsibilities and to possess the courage to forge ahead against the greatest of obstacles. We feel that the present crisis will be met with fortitude and somehow, some way, our brothers on the farm will come up with the answers to their problems.*
>
> *In the days ahead new barns, new homes and new equipment will rise from the ruins that came to many of our great Boone County farms. Help will be given by all, neighbors and city folk, government and disaster funds. The American farm cannot and will not be let down by any American worthy of his name.*

Jim Turner, whose home on Lawrenceville Road was demolished by the tornado, is one of those farmers. "We had so much help from the community and from everyplace else," he said. "We had a group of Mennonites come up with a camper and stay at our neighbors' [property]. They helped tear out all of the windows of my old house." Later, said Jim, the Mennonites stayed and worked for him at his shop.

"Dick Thomas, who was on the county board and was the head of the disaster team, and Jerry Maars, our road commissioner, got some federal help," Jim recalled.

Jim said that after the tornado, trucks and crawlers tore down what was left of the buildings and hauled them away to gravel pits. "The EPA and health department would have [had] a heart attack over that today," Jim said. "But we got cleaned up, and we moved on with our lives.

"Some other people that need to be recognized are the Cordray brothers, Jim and Buck, and Pop, their dad. These guys were here with heavy equipment and worked in our neighborhood for months, and they never were compensated. A good dinner and a pat on the back is all these guys ever got, but they were really good people. The community owes them a big thank-you."

Jim, like others, can't thank everyone. But there is one person or family whom he thinks about to this day. "I'd like to thank somebody, and I don't know who I'm thanking," he said. "Somebody sent us $500, sent our family $500…to help with our problems. To this day, I've never been able to thank them because I don't know who it was."

Chapter 13

HELPING BECOMES SECOND NATURE

It is impossible to tell all the stories of those who helped others that day—before, during and after the killer twister hit Belvidere. Four of the most recent stories to surface involve selfless acts, small kindnesses and seemingly routine experiences.

Pam (Wilson) Damm also rode the only bus that left before the storm struck. Like Karen Cross described in chapter 10, she looked out the bus window and saw the tornado to the south and was later dropped off at Perry School. Pam was surprised to see her father, a Belvidere police officer, there to pick her up. He never picked her up because the family lived only a block from Perry School. But her dad wanted to ensure her safety, so he was there that day. Once home, her father checked to make sure her younger brother and sister—who were in junior high—were in the house; they had walked home and were fine. Pam's father then changed into his uniform "and went into the thick of it."

This was the late 1960s. There was no Internet, no Twitter, no text messages, so Pam doesn't know how her father found out about the tornado. "We didn't know what was going on," she said. "We knew there was a storm, but we didn't know there were any problems. I don't know if they had an all-call from the police department to get all of the officers on duty, but he knew something. I'm guessing that he got a phone call."

Belvidere police officer Charles Wilson, who supervised the rescue effort at the Belvidere High School gym, is shown in this photo taken prior to the tornado. *Courtesy of Wilson family.*

As soon as he knew his children were safe, Officer Charles Wilson, a fourteen-year veteran of the Belvidere Police Department, went to work. Charles—who had two nicknames, "Chuck" and "Bud"—went straight to the high school. "He was put in charge of the gymnasium, which they were using as a morgue," Pam said. "It was heart-wrenching for Dad. [He said] it was very, very difficult. He said he had to keep people out." Pam recalled her father telling her about a mother and father in a desperate search. "He said one couple came in and found their child [dead]....It was devastating," she said.

The memories weighed heavily on Officer Wilson. Tragedy soon struck the family. In the summer of 1967, only months after the tornado and the stressful duties it had required of him, Officer Wilson had a heart attack. He recovered and went back to work by Christmas 1967 but did not survive another heart attack in January 1968.

Seven children who rode the Caledonia bus were killed that day. Two brothers who rode the same bus—Kraig Bryan, fourteen, and Kurt Bryan, twelve—escaped with relatively minor injuries. Kraig got off the bus and was running to the school when he was knocked to the ground. He suffered cuts and bruises and had a three-inch piece of wood driven into his back. Kurt, unable to get off, was cut badly on his scalp. "The bus rolled over six times," said their mother, Elizabeth Harris. "The bus driver ordered the children off. And some of them were killed when they got off." Unable to open the emergency door, Kurt stayed with the bus, which rolled over at least six times.

After the tornado, Kraig helped Steven Chance, fourteen, a friend and neighbor who suffered two broken legs. In a *Rockford Morning Star* news story, photos show Kraig, who weighed 190 pounds, lifting Steven from his wheelchair into a go-cart that Kraig built for him. The story reported that Kraig "lifts Steve out of his wheelchair and into the go-cart and back again as gently as one would handle a baby. When Kraig pushes Steve around in his wheelchair, it's not just a pleasant stroll. Kraig tips the wheelchair back so the front wheels are off the ground, and they're off on a brisk trot."

Because of his injuries, Steven was unable to return to school that spring and was taught by a tutor. Before the tornado, he had played football and gone out for track. "But I guess the closest I'll get to football this fall will be the rooting section," he told the newspaper.

Power outages and communication breakdowns commonly occur after major storms. Less than twenty-four hours after the tornado struck, emergency crews had restored most vital services to Belvidere residents.

By 1:00 p.m. on Saturday, April 22, Commonwealth Edison not only had restored electrical service to the city but had also brought back power to the main well, which allowed the pumping station to provide safe water to homes. A boil-water warning had been in effect. By nightfall, all habitable dwellings had power and at least one cold water tap.

Sometimes lost in the complexity of a recovery of services are stories of what people did to help others. Ivan Dye had such a story of a day that began routinely. "Friday, April 21, 1967, started as a normal workday," said Ivan, who worked for the GTE telephone company, located at the southeast corner of Locust and South State Streets. His job was to maintain the telephone equipment, which allowed customers using the rotary phones common at that time to complete calls. "As telephones were removed from their cradles, equipment was seized and prepared to receive commands transmitted by the dial impulses from the fingers of the dialer," he said. The building Ivan worked in was enclosed with no windows, so he had no idea of the weather conditions that day. Besides, he said, "our work allowed little time to look outside." However, in the mid-afternoon, he received a call from a fellow GTE employee who asked if he had peered outside recently. When he did, he saw hail stones "as large as golf balls bouncing across the parking lot. I saw…a black curtain filled with debris flying through the air a few blocks south."

About ten minutes later, his normal workday changed abruptly. "The telephone equipment crashed as hundreds of people had all lifted their telephone receivers at the same time, locking the equipment," he said. That meant that no calls could be made in Belvidere. Quickly, he and his co-workers sprang into action, without knowing what exactly had occurred. "We started opening up cable pairs by the dozens, trying to relieve the load on the equipment, enough to where the unaffected people could get dial tones and call out," he said. When he realized what area had been affected, "we had to completely open up the cables going south to give the rest of the town telephone service."

His quick action kept the lines of communication open at a time when the exchange of information was a matter of life and death.

Nothing seemed out of place when Sandra (Mallett) Gray boarded bus No. 16 at Belvidere High School with her brother Dan Mallett, seventeen, and sister Pam, fourteen. When Nick, their driver, steered the bus around a curve, everything changed. The riders were pelted with glass that had been blown out, along with tar and stones. The bus rolled and then landed upside down. Sandra was knocked unconscious, waking to find her legs pinned under window frames. Feeling no pain, she pulled herself out and exited the bus. "There was a small boy, covered in blood, standing near the bus crying," she said. "I picked him up and carried him into the building past what looked like a junkyard—the student parking lot." They went to the cafeteria, where, she recalled, "someone lit a lighter, and he was abruptly tackled. Everyone was afraid of gas leaks." She and her sister found rags, wet them and cleaned the little boy. It turned out he had minor scrapes. Most of the blood on him wasn't his.

"I found my sister, who was complaining of her shoulder hurting," Sandra said. "I told her to quit being dramatic, only to find out later she had a broken collarbone and deep gashes on her knee." When they realized that their brother wasn't with them, Sandra could only recall that he had a gash on the side of his head. He had been thrown from the bus and was taken to St. Joseph's Hospital. There, he was told to wait, but he agreed to ride with someone who offered to take him to Rockford Memorial Hospital. Doctors found he had both hips broken—one horizontally, one vertically—and a concussion. He was hospitalized for several weeks and spent most of that summer on crutches.

Sandra and Pam later boarded a bus being used as an ambulance. "We dropped our worst cases—the ones on doors rather than stretchers—at St. Anthony's," she said. But because the hospital was full, they moved on to Swedish-American. "But they also were full," she said. Next stop: Rockford Memorial Hospital, where their bus was the first to arrive. There they lined up to wait for treatment.

At this point, her story took a dramatic turn. "A very strange-looking man with his glasses down his nose, his hair messy and [with] multiple cameras hanging around his neck walked down the line, pointed and said he [wanted] the selected individuals cleaned and put on his docket," Sandra said. "Luckily, I was one of the selected group." A nurse took a basin of hot, soapy water and, using a scrub brush and sponges, cleaned the open wounds on her legs. When this happened, she said, it brought her out of shock. "I saw the reason he had selected me," she said. "The side of my lower leg was basically gone. The tar and debris had stopped the normal blood flow, and since it didn't hurt, I didn't notice it."

She was taken into surgery, where the man took more photos of her legs and prepared her for anesthesia. "He asked if I would like to hear Shakespeare or a gory poem while he worked on me," she said. "I chose

Shakespeare since I had [had] enough gore. When he dismissed me, my right leg was wrapped from thigh to foot and my left leg [on both sides of the knee]." She was told not to walk for two weeks.

Her father, who saw the storm while working on a building roof near the Kishwaukee River, and her mother finally found all three children about 10:00 p.m. at Rockford Memorial. When Sandra went in for a follow-up visit with her doctor, she discovered that the "strange-looking man" was Dr. Hugh H. Johnson, a Rockford plastic surgeon. "He had come in, chosen the tornado victims he thought needed his type of surgery and forgave any charges that the insurance company did not pay," Sandra said. "He worked in Rockford for twenty-seven years and in missionary efforts as a plastic surgeon working with lepers in India and civilian war victims in Vietnam. A year after the tornado, he performed reconstructive surgery on my sister, Pam West [also from our bus], and myself with the same payment forgiveness."

Sandra is unsure how many other Belvidere Tornado victims benefited from Dr. Johnson's skill and generosity. "But he was a man to be remembered, and I always will be grateful he picked me to work on," she said.

Chapter 14

THOSE WHO WERE LOST

It took only about ten minutes. Yet in that time, the vicious Belvidere Tornado took twenty-four lives, many of them children. It's hard to imagine the anguish of friends and family members as they desperately searched for their loved ones, only to find that they had not survived.

In the April 24, 1967 edition of the *Monday Morning Mail*, a weekly newspaper in Loves Park, Illinois, Stanley Haines described the ordeal he and his wife experienced while searching for their daughter Pamela Haines, who was fourteen years old when she died. Stanley and Virginia looked for three hours, first going to Belvidere Junior High School, then to the high school, then to St. Anthony Hospital. "All the parents were suffering such anguish, trying to get information on their children," Stanley said. "And there was no one central source of information to go to. It was all so chaotic." Stanley and Virginia finally took a grim trip to Whitbeck-Wheeler-Sabien Funeral Home in Belvidere, where they found their daughter, Pamela.

The first book we wrote about the Belvidere Tornado in 2007 featured a list of the twenty-four casualties with scant information about most of the victims. For this edition, we have attempted to provide more details, using as many resources as possible. We hope this provides a better picture of the people who lost their lives on April 21, 1967, so that they are more than just names in a book or on a monument.

Michael Bates, Six

Michael, son of Richard and Loretta Bates, was a first-grade student at Lincoln School. He had one brother, Robert. He was born in Belvidere and lived his entire life there. He was a member of First Methodist Church. Recently, his mother, Loretta Bates, wrote this:

> *Friday, April 21, 1967. That morning started out as a beautiful spring day.*
>
> *But ended being life changing…My first born son Michael was killed on a school bus at the high school.*
>
> *Michael was six, a first-grader at Lincoln School. Michael had just gotten a brand new 2-wheel bike and learned to ride. He was anxious to get home after school, to get riding. That morning he begged me to pick him up after school so that he didn't have to ride the bus. I said OK because I was going to have the car.*
>
> *We only had one car, and usually my husband took it to work. But this day our water heater element burned out. I was to get the part, so my husband could fix it on his lunch hour. After it was fixed at noon, he was late.* [So] *he took the car to get back to work.*
>
> *At the time that wasn't a problem because I could put my three-year-old son Robert in the stroller and go to Lincoln School and get him. About 3:00 I started walking and noticed to the south a storm was rolling in. I went back home and called school about 3:15 and told them to have him ride the bus.*
>
> *If only I'd have known! I never knew they picked up Lincoln School kids and then went to the high school to pick up kids.*
>
> *For many years, I've dealt with the guilt. It's been very challenging.*
>
> *My faith has made me strong and my son Michael forgave me and helped me forgive myself. Life-changing things happen.*

School photo of Michael Bates. *Courtesy of Bates family.*

To me losing one of your children at any age is something you never really recover from. You just learn to live with the ache. Life is precious.
—Loretta Bates, mom of Michael, Robert and Rita Beard

Cindy Day, Nine

Cindy was a third grader at Lincoln School. She had a sister, Mary Lou, and a brother, Ronald. The family had lived in Belvidere only two months, formerly residing in Cherry Valley, Sterling and Rock Falls. She was also survived by her parents, Ronald and Ruth Day.

Lawrence Decker, Seventeen

A student at Belvidere High School, the seventeen-year-old formerly attended St. James School. He was survived by his parents, Lloyd and Marcella Decker; sisters, Barbara Jo and Lori Ann; and brother, Terry.

Cecelia Eakin, Eighty-Three

Cecelia was from Cherry Valley. She was a patient at Highland Hospital before being transferred to St. Anthony, where she died at 7:00 p.m. on April 21.

Kent Ferguson, Twelve

Kent would have turned thirteen on April 22, 1967, the day after the tornado. The twelve-year-old was on the Caledonia bus when he was hit by debris caused by the tornado. He lived in rural Caledonia and was a member of the Cherry Valley Trail Ride Club, 4-H and the Junior Holstein-Friesian Association. He had a brother, Scott, and three sisters, Martha, Nadeen and Becky Lynn. He was also survived by his parents, Mr. and Mrs. Wilbur Ferguson.

Harold Gustafson, Seventy-Two

Harold, a retired farmer and longtime Boone County resident, was working at DeWane's when the tornado hit. He was a member of Zion Lutheran Church and the Boone County Farm Bureau. He was survived by his son, Donald, and daughter, Dorothy Rehn. His wife, Minnie, died in 1960.

Pamela Haines, Fourteen

Pamela was sitting in front of Dennis Norem on the Caledonia bus when she got off the bus and was killed. Her father, Stanley Haines, told the *Monday Morning Mail* of Loves Park that "five of her close friends also were killed trying to get out [of the bus]." Pamela was found lying near the buses by her cousin Bruce Juhlin. The family lived in rural Belvidere for two and a half years. She was a member of St. James Church and 4-H. She also was survived by her mother, Virginia Haines, and sister, Kimberly.

Mary Jean Hamre, Sixty-Five

Mary Jean died on her sixty-fifth birthday. She was returning from a birthday celebration in Dundee, Illinois, where she had been born in 1902. The group pulled into DeWane's, where the car she was riding in was hit by debris. Mary Jean taught at Stark Station and Berwyn for several years and then worked in the offices at the National Sewing Machine Company in Belvidere and National Lock Company in Rockford. She left a husband, Edward, three sisters and a brother. Edward died just over a year later on May 17, 1968.

Craig Hyser, Eight

Craig was from Garden Prairie and was a third grader at Washington School.

Barbara Johnson, Ten

Barbara was a fourth grade student at St. James School. She had two brothers, Gerald and Donald Jr. Her parents were Donald and Maxine Johnson. She had lived in Garden Prairie for fourteen months after moving from Rockford. She turned ten on April 10, 1967.

Gilbert Julin, Sixty-Three

Gilbert was a bus driver who was born in Caledonia. He was the chairman of the Boone County Zoning Board of Appeals, the Bonus Township tax assessor and a member and past trustee of Zion Lutheran Church. He was survived by his wife, Mildred, and two daughters, Sandra Cregeen and Mary Wirth.

After Gilbert retired from his full-time job as tax assessor, he continued to work part time. He was a mail driver for the U.S. Postal Service, chopped and sold wood from the woods on his farm and sold seed corn. But perhaps his favorite and most meaningful job was as a bus driver. "Every day he drove the bus, he wore dress pants," his daughter, the late Sandra Cregeen, said. "People have told me: 'Your dad was always dressed up.'" Cregeen said that before the tornado, her dad had expressed sorrow about having to give up his bus driving route. He would tell Sandra, "'What am I going to do without the kids?' He was that attached to them," she said.

Gilbert's back problem, a slipped disc, kept him from driving the week of the tornado and the week before. A relative, Randolph Reed, had taken his route. About 2:00 p.m. on April 21, 1967, Gilbert got a call from the bus dispatcher telling him that Randolph had to take another bus and that they needed him to work, Sandra recalled. "Otherwise, he would have been at home."

Gilbert's bus route covered rural areas east of Belvidere along Lawrenceville Road. One of his regular riders was Teri (Turner) Keegan, a fourteen-year-old Belvidere High School freshman. "He was my bus driver since I was in kindergarten," Teri said. "He was a very kind man."

The bus was toward the front of the line of those waiting to turn onto East Avenue. When the storm approached, Teri said that Gilbert yelled to the students on his crowded bus, "Get down and put your hands over your head! It's a tornado!"

Gilbert then turned on the interior lights of the bus so the children wouldn't be scared. The tremendous winds rocked the bus before rolling it over. During the storm, a board smashed through the windshield, striking Gilbert's back and killing him. "A little boy was found alive underneath him," Sandra said. "We were very proud of him."

Bruce Lindley, Thirteen

Bruce had just boarded the Caledonia bus with his brother, Doug, fifteen, when the bus driver spotted the tornado and told the students to run to the high school. As Bruce fled for safety, he was "caught by the tornado and hurled to his death," according to the *Rockford Morning Star*. Doug had been unable to get out of the bus and was trapped while it rolled three times, suffering lacerations, the worst a badly cut knee. Bruce also was survived by his parents, Jack and Adah Lindley, and two sisters, Judy and Pamela. He was a member of Willow Creek Presbyterian Church and the Caledonia Trail Blazers 4-H Club.

Adah Maurine Lindley Lepp, Bruce's mother, wrote this memorial that appeared in the *Rockford Register Star* on April 30, 2007:

> *The girls and I waited at our Caledonia bus stop for their brothers, Doug and Bruce, to drive them home in the rain. I went down to meet the bus that afternoon because I had bought new shoes for the boys and I didn't want them to get dirty from the recent rain. The bus never came. Why? We learned a tornado had hit the buses at Belvidere High School. Where were they? We waited and hoped for a phone call while their Dad and Granddaddy started searching. A Rockford friend answered my radio broadcast plea of: "Have you seen them?" with the news that Doug was at Swedish American Hospital and he was OK. We were so thankful!*
>
> *But where was Bruce?* [After] *many hours of frantically searching area hospitals and the makeshift morgue at the high school, his Dad and a friend knew there was only one other place to look. They found him in the main funeral parlor. He was washed clean. The other casualties were covered in mud and dirt. I never knew why until a year later. A nurse at the doctor's office asked, "Didn't you lose a son in the tornado?" The nurse said she was in the operating room for hours with Bruce and he never regained consciousness. Flying glass had hit him in the temple as he was getting off the bus, trying to get to the high school.*

Left: Bruce Lindley's school photo. *Courtesy of Pam Lindley*.

Below: The Lindley family. *Courtesy of Pam Lindley*.

> *Bruce's English teacher put it so aptly when she shared with us a poem he had recently written. The teacher said, "This shows what a fine and wholesome boy Bruce was. We all loved and respected him and miss him." Even after these many years, our whole family still feels the loss of someone so dear.*

Bruce is most likely the victim described by St. Joseph Hospital nurse Norma Duclon, who earlier recalled how doctors fought to keep a boy with "crushing injuries to his head" alive. Norma said that as the boy was taken to the morgue, she wept.

This poem was written by Bruce in his English class shortly before he was killed. His teacher shared it with Bruce's parents after the tragedy:

> *"Happiness Is"*
> *Happiness is the feeling of satisfaction and pleasure, giving and receiving presents, working on your favorite hobby, being complimented on a report.*
> *Happiness is the expression on someone's face when you tell him a joke, having a good time at a party,*
> *walking through a beautiful garden, smelling the air after it rained.*
> *Happiness is seeing your family after a long trip, when school is ended, and in the summer when it is hot, a boat ride in the summer on a hot day.*
> *—Bruce Edward Lindley, age 13*

Cristine Lutzow, Nine

The youngest of four, Cristine had two older brothers, Harlan and Lawrence, and a sister, Donna. Harlan was serving in the U.S. Army in Vietnam at the time, while Donna was a student nurse at St. Anthony Hospital. Cristine was the daughter of Mr. and Mrs. Everett Lutzow.

Sandra McLain, Twenty-One

Sandra was the wife of Robert McLain, a Belvidere fireman. Born in Alabama, she married Robert in Rockford. She left a son, Kevin, eighteen months, and a daughter, Karen, eight months. According to the *Belvidere Daily Republican*, she died of injuries suffered at the Pacemaker Food Store.

Theodore Nelson, Fifteen

Ted was the son of a teacher, Margaret Nelson, who taught at Maple School in the Harlem School District. Ted was on the Caledonia bus. Born in Rockford, he was a freshman at Belvidere High School and a member of St. James Catholic Church in Belvidere. He had two brothers, Gregory and Lawrence (Larry), and two sisters, Sandra Ann (Sandee) and Theresa (Teri). He also was survived by his father, LaVern Nelson. Recently, his brother Larry wrote this tribute:

> *My name is Larry Nelson. In April 1967, I was 19 years old living at home in Caledonia with my parents and three of my four siblings, Sandee, Ted, and Teri. I was attending Rock Valley College in Rockford, Illinois. On April 21, 1967, I spent the afternoon in the Rockford Public Library doing research for a paper that was due at the end of the semester. There was a brief power outage that resulted in two elderly women being stuck in an elevator for about five minutes. They were hysterical and the library staff* [was] *trying to calm them. The power was restored and the women recovered their composure. When I was done, I left the library and headed home.*
>
> *While I was on Illinois* [Route] *173 going through the Beloit Road intersection, the local radio station announced that a tornado had hit Belvidere. I experienced a momentary clammy feeling. When I reached Caledonia, there were several residents congregated across the street from Caledonia Grade School. They were discussing the tornado and waiting for the missing to return via Caledonia Road. There was one father who was almost hysterical with glee when he learned that his son had skipped school that day and was safe. He stated that his son could skip school anytime. Within an hour, my parents and my sister*

School photo of Ted Nelson. *Courtesy of Nelson family.*

Sandee arrived. Sandee was muddied and bruised. She was on a school bus that was hit by the tornado and rolled over several times, landing in the field where a school now stands. They were very distraught because they could not find Ted. I told them that two of my friends and I would go back to Belvidere and find Ted.

When we arrived in Belvidere, it was like a war zone. There were National Guard, police, and firemen everywhere. We drove as far as we could and then proceeded on foot. We found out that the Community Building was where all the students were being kept until somebody claimed them. We went to the Community Building and tried to find Ted. We were unsuccessful. I inquired as to where the deceased were being kept. I was told that a temporary morgue had been set up at the Whitbeck, Wheeler and Sabin Funeral Home on Logan Avenue, about three blocks from the Community Building.

Upon arriving at the funeral home, we were advised that the temporary morgue was located in the garage. Upon entering the garage, there were several bodies with white plastic sheets over and under them. I gave them a description of Ted and they took us to the deceased boys. They would lift the top sheet so the face was visible. I was watching one of my friend's face for a reaction. When we got to Ted, his expression changed. I looked down and initially thought he was mistaken because this person had a full face and Ted was thin and angular. Upon further examination, I realized that it was Ted with a swollen face from the trauma. I was in total shock. I went out on the porch of the funeral home and cried uncontrollably. Once I regained some composure, I asked to use a phone to call my parents. I was escorted to the basement to a phone. My mom answered the phone and I asked to talk to dad. She became hysterical. My dad took the phone and I told him I had found Ted and he was dead.

From talking to my sister Sandee and others, I concluded that Ted was on the same bus as Sandee. He was closer to the door and able to exit the bus. He was hit by the tornado as he was running toward the school. His body was found on the roof of the school.

David Wayne Poe, Thirteen

David, of rural Belvidere, was survived by his parents, Mr. and Mrs. Wayne Poe, and four siblings: a brother, Darrell, and sisters Debra Ann, Diana Lynn and Darla Kay. His services were held in DeKalb.

Dwight David Shaw, Eleven

Dwight was on the Caledonia bus. He was a fourth grade student at Washington School and had five siblings: Lester, Dennis, Lois Thustad, Susan Erickson and Tammy Shaw. Born in Rochelle, his family moved to Belvidere in 1957. He was also survived by his parents, Dwight Leslie and Jean Shaw.

Timothy Smith, Seventeen

A junior at Belvidere High School, Tim was on the Caledonia bus. Tim was a good student, excelling in math. He was blind in one eye and couldn't see very well, but he was exceptionally smart. He survived for about a week before passing away. One of his best friends was Ted Nelson. He was survived by his parents, Jim and Genela Smith, and siblings Eloise, Ann, Arlene, Steve, George, Rodney and Theresa.

Vicky Jo Smith, Nine

A Lincoln School student, Vicky was killed on a bus. She lived in Poplar Grove with her mother, Joyce McCain. She also was survived by her father, Willie Smith.

Jack Stoll, Twenty-Three

Jack was an assistant manager at Pacemaker Food Store and a member of the Cherry Valley Volunteer Fire Department. According to the *Rockford Morning Star*, Jack left to answer a fire alarm in Cherry Valley and was killed in his vehicle during the tornado. Originally from Waterloo, Iowa, Jack had lived in Cherry Valley near the intersection of State Street and Mill Road for two years, moving there from Sterling. He left his wife, Shirley, and three sons, Michael, Randall and Terry.

Johnnie Tate, Six

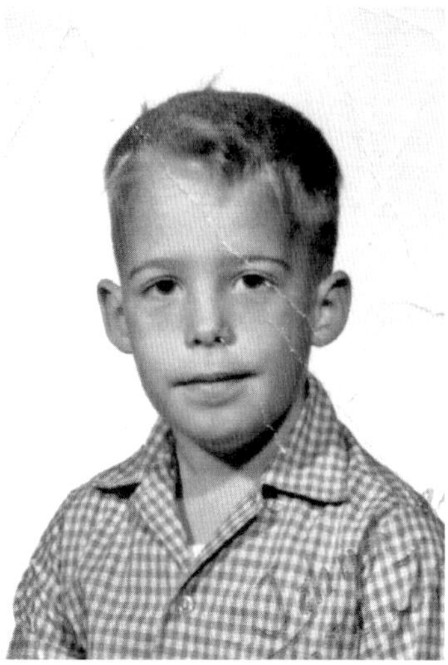

Johnnie Tate. *Courtesy of Tate family.*

A first grader at Washington School, Johnnie lived all of his life in Belvidere. He left his parents, John and Evelyn Tate, and four sisters, Sandra Schultz, Donna Chilson, Carol Tate and Judy Tate.

On August 26, 1967, A.J. Crawford (whose son married Johnnie Tate's sister after Johnnie died) wrote this to the *Belvidere Daily Republican*:

> *April 21 1967: Bulletin reports be on the lookout for bad storms in the Northern Illinois area. Thirty-eight tornadoes touched down. Belvidere hit hard; shopping center, Highland hospital, new high school area hit hard as students were entering buses.*
>
> *Feeling so helpless, I could only pray for all that need help; that each would have the strength that it takes, that we have the help to understand that it is only as far away as the asking. Give us the privilege to give the right word to the right person at the right time. Let us give each what they seek—other than what we think they should have, and to lend a smile to those whom have lost it.*
>
> *When my son and his fiancé, who is now my daughter-in-law, asked me, "Why?" I was very thankful I had already wrote the above with the aid of an oil lantern and a battery radio some thoughtful soul brought me.*
>
> *"JOHNNIE," one of many victims of the storm could have been your child or mine who gave his all, let it all not be in vain, but let it remind us to make this a better and safer community. That each of us as a citizen are guilty of neglect to have allowed such a mass catastrophe.*
>
> *With the permission of Mr. and Mrs. John Tate, I wish to present this to the public.*
>
> *"When Johnnie's Not Away"*
>
> *It was the twenty-first of April*
> *The clouds were suddenly gray,*

They reached down on the school
Johnnie was taken away.
We will not forget the day
When the Master called the clay,
Johnnie went on ahead
So we might find the way.
He graduated from his school
With highest honors on his scroll,
The highest role of all
When he answered to the call
Why! Was I to stay behind
The answer not hard to find
For Johnnie was at that time
Who was not to stay behind.
So humbly I pray oh LORD
When I may know the day,
That I may go on ahead
And Johnnie's not away.

Phyllis Van Brocklin, Thirteen

Phyllis also was sitting behind Dennis Norem on the Caledonia bus when she died. She was an eighth grader at Belvidere Junior High School, where she was an honor student. She lived in rural Caledonia and was involved in 4-H as a member of the Caledonia Star Dusters 4-H Club. She also was a member of the Boone County Horse and Pony Club. She was survived by her parents, Orville and Mary Van Brocklin. She had one sister, Alice, who was working at Belvidere National Bank that Friday afternoon. Alice saw the storm and recalled thinking about Phyllis. "I was trying to calculate in my mind where she was," Alice said. Phyllis had just finished her day at Belvidere Junior High School and was on a bus that would have taken her to her rural Caledonia home. "She was a straight-A student," Alice says. "She wanted to be a veterinarian."

Rebecca Vogelsang, Eight

Rebecca was a student at Immanuel Lutheran. She was born in Fresno, California. She left parents Clarence and Alma Vogelsang; three brothers, Nathan, Danny and Roger; and two sisters, Elsa and Helena. The Reverend Eugene Wille, former pastor at Immanuel Lutheran and a tornado survivor, remembered that day and the day that Rebecca was buried, Wednesday, April 26, 1967. "I'll never forget her funeral service," he said. "Her second grade classmates from Immanuel sang for Becky. They were in the balcony, and they sang, 'I am Jesus' Little Lamb.'"

Norine Wych, Eighty-One

Norine died at the home of her daughter Novella Wilson of Belvidere, of an apparent heart attack as she watched the storm. She lived in Garden Prairie for forty-four years and was the widow of John G. Wych. Born in Rockford, she was active in the Garden Prairie United Church of Christ. She was survived by three other daughters, Myrtle Peters, Elizabeth Smith and Marilyn Orr, as well as thirty-two grandchildren and fourteen great-grandchildren.

In memory of the three children of employees of the Belvidere Assembly Plant who were killed on April 21, 1967—David Wayne Poe, Cindy Ruth Day and Lawrence Eugene Decker—the Chrysler Corporation donated two school buses to Belvidere CUSD 100.

Chapter 15

THREE MORE TORNADOES

At first, no one could believe it. It was the end of the day on January 7, 2008, when the tornado alarm sounded at Belvidere North High School and those students and staff members still in the building were ordered to report to the nearest tornado shelter. After all, it was January. There were never any tornadoes in January. Even though the day had been unseasonably warm, reaching sixty-three degrees, this seemed absurd. Until you looked at the sky.

As students and teachers sat on hallway floors, unsure of what was occurring, two teachers watched weather reports of the storm on the computer monitor in art teacher Troy Yunk's room. The windows in his room faced northwest, and what they saw awed them. They were looking at the dark storm that became the Poplar Grove Tornado.

According to the National Weather Service, it was a rare winter tornado. The weather event was "unusually intense and climatologically very rare," the service reported. In its fifty-eight years of compiling weather data, the service said it was only the second tornado reported in northern Illinois in January.

The irony of this event was not lost on those at the high school. Like the April 21, 1967 tornado at Belvidere High School, events took place at the end of a school day. Also, the 1967 tornado struck BHS in its first year of operation; Belvidere North had also opened its doors at the start of the 2007–8 school year. But unlike the 1967 event, this storm touched down farther north.

Damage sustained to Edwards Apple Orchard, a popular regional attraction, on January 7, 2008. *Courtesy of Bob Edwards.*

An aerial photo of a home severely damaged by the Fairdale Tornado. *Courtesy of Dave Ernest.*

As fate would have it, two more tornadoes have struck in the Boone County area: the Caledonia Tornado of November 22, 2010, and the Fairdale Tornado of April 9, 2015, when two women, next-door neighbors, were killed.

As residents of Boone County can attest, there is no such thing as tornado season. Hardly a week goes by when some place in the United States has not been struck a devastating weather-related blow, whether from hurricanes or tornadoes. However, in most cases, there is not the tremendous loss of life that occurred in Belvidere in 1967. Among the reasons are improvements in forecasting models, placement of tornado sirens and better communication methods, such as modern cellphone technology, which can provide effective early warning to residents in tornadoes' dangerous paths.

The Poplar Grove Tornado

Conditions more typical of early May brought severe weather to northern Illinois that day in early January. The tornado started about a mile north of Poplar Grove at about 3:30 p.m.—thirty-five minutes after the new chimes signaled the end of the day at Belvidere North High School. By 3:48 p.m., it ended in McHenry County about three miles northeast of Harvard. In its path was Edwards Apple Orchard, one of Boone County's most iconic and popular destinations.

Edwards Apple Orchard attracts about 225,000 visitors each fall. The orchard began in 1963 when Bob and Betty Edwards bought the property on Centerville Road, then a dairy farm, from Bob's parents and began to plant apple trees. The milk cow barn became the Apple Barn, a retail shop, and other outbuildings became attractions that began to draw visitors from not only the Rockford area but metropolitan Chicago as well. In time, Bob and Betty transferred ownership to Barb and Ken Hall, their daughter and son-in-law. Over the years, going to Edwards has become an autumn tradition in Boone County, as visitors seek out its freshly made apple cider doughnuts, apple-picking opportunities and family-friendly atmosphere.

On January 7, 2008, everything changed for Edwards Apple Orchard, which was struck by an EF3 tornado. At about 3:35 p.m., the tornado touched down northeast of Poplar Grove, west of the intersection of Centerville and Beaverton Roads. It continued past Stimes and North Boone School Roads as it moved toward Harvard in McHenry County. In its wake, thirty-eight structures were damaged, including barns, outbuildings, silos, garages and seventeen homes. Four homes were destroyed, four had major damage and nine had minor damage. Nine vehicles were damaged, and one horse was killed.

"It could have been any of our houses," Kelly Reininger said in the *Rockford Register Star*. Her neighbor's home was leveled, trapping two people in the basement, according to Boone County sheriff's deputies.

The tornado also swept through Chuck Kastning's dairy farm on Capron Road, and its fury caused six thousand households to lose power.

Its most well-known target, though, was Edwards Apple Orchard, located on Centerville Road just west of Beaverton. There were no injuries, but the damage was significant.

Ken and Barb Hall were at their home on the orchard property when the tornado struck. According to WREX (the local NBC affiliate), Barb and their son made it to the basement, but Ken was stuck in a staircase on the second floor. "[The house] rocked on its foundation and the superstructure is ruined," Ken said. "But the family's OK, our neighbors are OK. Even our dog Oli showed up a few minutes later."

The barn, which housed the gift shop, bakery and snack bar, was severely damaged, as was the adjacent building with its apple- and apple cider–processing facilities. The house lost its front porch roof and had damage to its roof and outside walls.

"I don't think any of the structures survived [intact]," Ken Hall said in the *Register Star*. However, the tornado spared the orchard's signature apple trees.

The response was immediate, as volunteers and others came to help restore Edwards. By the fall of 2008, it was again open for business.

Said Barb Hall in a statement:

> *Like everyone in our community who was impacted by the tornado, we were astonished by the amount of support and incredible kindness shown by our community. Family, neighbors, students, businesses, organizations, churches, fire and sheriff departments, Com Ed, and even strangers would just show up and start helping. Even now, many years later, it brings tears to my eyes to think of the goodness of so many people. We are different people than before the storm. We no longer sweat the small stuff, but, most importantly, we have a greater awareness of how extraordinarily kind and compassionate people and communities are to those in need.*

The Caledonia Tornado

It was November 22, 2010, the Monday of Thanksgiving week, a time of year when temperatures in the upper fifties and low sixties were unexpected, with high humidity. They were the result of strong southerly winds that drew Rick Walraven outside to do some yard work, despite his foot surgery two days earlier. "I was supposed to be taking it easy," Rick said. "But Monday afternoon was so beautiful I just couldn't sit around." A neighbor joined Rick and his father at his Caledonia home to do some yard work. "I supervised," Rick said. At about 2:30 p.m., a hard rain started, so the group dispersed. "My dad lived in Belvidere, and he saw a very dark cloud in the southwest," Rick said. "But he really didn't think anything of it." Rick was inside when the rain began falling harder. Then he heard an ominous sound. "I could hear the tornado coming down the street," he said. "Everyone says it sounds like a train, but to me, it sounded like a two-thousand-horsepower Hoover vacuum cleaner. I don't know how I knew it was a tornado. I just knew."

Relying on his instincts—Caledonia did not have tornado sirens at that time—Rick ran toward the basement. "I made it as far as the dining room when the front windows blew out and the front door blew in," he said. "I knew I couldn't make it to the basement, so I went into a cove in the kitchen and held on for dear life."

From his kitchen, Rick watched as the tornado aimed for his garage. "After the windows had blown out, there was a lot of pressure—all the air was sucked out of my lungs," he said. "I heard the roof rip and then the back wall. It was all I could do to hold on—the wind was so strong. I had a five- by eight-foot trailer parked next to the garage. [The tornado] went up the side of the garage to the peak and down the street."

The three-thousand-pound boat in Rick's driveway shifted about twenty feet to its side. "We had just finished putting insulation in the house, and it was stuck all over everything, including me," he said. "Then there was silence. No birds. Nothing but eerie silence."

Rick emerged from his house to find others outside, including a man walking up his driveway. "He was talking on his cellphone, [and since] mine was missing, he was kind enough to let me use it to call my wife, Mary, who was working for the North Boone School District," he said. When Mary tried to get home, she found her path blocked by emergency vehicles and downed power lines, so she had to walk several blocks. When she got home, she found it had been destroyed.

"My guardian angel must have been watching over me because our house was one of [six] that were totally demolished, and I was not injured," Rick said. Before she left that day, Mary had placed on the counter next to the stove several canisters to be decorated. Next to them was a full bag of potato chips. The granite backsplash from the kitchen and the home's roof were found 160 feet away. "But the canisters and the potato chips were still on the counter," Rick said.

The tornado was the result of the collision of the warm southerly winds with a massive cold front led by thunderstorms. The storm began in extreme eastern Winnebago County at 3:04 p.m. About a mile east of Rock Cut State Park and near the intersection of Argyle and Harlem Roads, a school bus was toppled and six on board were injured. After knocking down eleven electrical high-tension towers nearby, the tornado moved into western Boone County across open fields until it struck Caledonia. According to the National Weather Service, six buildings in Caledonia had significant damage, with another twenty with minor damage. Several large trees were snapped or uprooted, and a grain bin was partially collapsed. Heading northeast, it downed power poles, blew off roofs and destroyed three farm outbuildings. One of these buildings, located two miles northwest of Capron, also had been damaged in the Poplar Grove Tornado of 2008. Designated an EF2 tornado, it did its most damage in Caledonia. By 3:23 p.m., the tornado had disappeared.

The Fairdale Tornado

The peak tornado season in Illinois runs from April through June, averaging forty a year. Since 1950, only thirty-three EF4 or stronger tornadoes are on record, including Belvidere on April 21, 1967, and Washington, Illinois, on November 17, 2013. The last EF4 tornado in northern Illinois was on August 28, 1990, at Plainfield. Until Fairdale.

Early on Saturday, April 4, 2015, the National Weather Service (NWS) posted the potential for severe weather in the area. Even with that prediction, few were prepared for what happened on April 9, 2015. "The atmosphere was ripe for severe weather due to highly anomalous moisture and instability for early April across the region," the National Weather Service reported. "A strong low pressure system advanced into this air mass. Combined with robust wind shear, this helped to trigger these potent storms."

The result was a super cell thunderstorm that produced eleven tornadoes, six of which were formed in north-central Illinois. The NWS defines super cell thunderstorms as uncommon, highly organized storms that can last for hours with updrafts and winds more than one hundred miles per hour. They are responsible for nearly all of the significant tornadoes in the United States

Above: Illinois governor Bruce Rauner greets a first responder at the one-year memorial in Fairdale on April 9, 2016. *Photo by Mike Doyle.*

Right: The remnants of a tree destroyed by the Fairdale Tornado house a memorial today. *Photo by Mike Doyle.*

and for most of the hailstones that are golf ball size or larger, according to the NWS. The tornado that struck Fairdale was EF4. It was the strongest of all the tornadoes that day. Formed near Franklin Grove in Lee County, it plowed through the northwest side of Rochelle in Ogle County, across Interstate 39 and through Fairdale in DeKalb County, where it killed two—Jackie Klosa and Geraldine "Geri" Schultz—and injured twenty-two. It finally lifted south of Belvidere. "A tornado of this magnitude is quite rare," the NWS reported.

Connie Hernandez Eloy and her husband lived in a ranch home north of Rochelle, off Route 251 and south of Route 64. Connie recalled a Rockford TV station telling viewers to take shelter if they lived between Ashton and Hillcrest. "We were in that path," said Connie, who looked outside to see a severe hailstorm and more. "There were numerous funnel clouds that all of a sudden went up into this huge cloud and came back down [as a tornado]," she said. The Loys gathered their cats and dogs and got to the basement just as the tornado hit the house. "It was just like they say—a train coming over us," Connie said. "There was lots of dust and insulation settling."

Connie and her husband were huddled in the dark basement as the tornado eased. Then they heard voices. "Our neighbors close by were yelling, 'Hello! Anybody down there? Are you OK?'" recalled Connie. "Then we saw this light on our staircase—and it was daylight." Their house was gone, with the only thing standing a section of the kitchen with the range. "We never did find anything," Connie said. The tornado also took out an outbuilding where her husband had a shop.

"We were not injured. We all were fine," she said. "But instantly, it seemed, there were like a million people around offering all kinds of help. We couldn't have done anything without the help from all of the strangers and others."

The Loys' house had the most damage in their neighborhood. "We're the first subdivision as you come from Ashton," she said. "We got hit before it hit Grubsteakers."

Grubsteakers was a family-style restaurant located at the northeast corner of Illinois Routes 251 and 64. Twelve people were in the restaurant when it took a direct hit from the tornado. All made it to the basement in time, but they had to be pulled from the wreckage afterward. Grubsteakers was rebuilt and reopened seventeen months later in September 2016.

The tornado continued churning on its menacing way to the northeast. By the time it got to Fairdale, about eight miles from the restaurant, it was so wide—seven hundred yards, nearly a half mile—that Kimberly Radostits could not actually see a funnel from her home. "It was just a big green strip," she said.

Kimberly, who teaches Spanish at Oregon High School, was in her classroom at about 5:30 p.m. that day when a friend popped in to tell her she should head home because a tornado watch had been posted for Oregon. She saw nothing unusual on her thirty-five-minute drive home to Fairdale. When she got home, she worked on lesson plans on her laptop for about twenty minutes and then began to prepare dinner for herself and her mother. Then she heard a warning on her radio that a tornado was headed toward Kirkland, about five miles east on Route 72.

"My mother and I went downstairs to the basement," Kimberly said. "We spent maybe five to six minutes [there], and nothing was happening. So we came upstairs, and I started cooking dinner because it just seemed normal." That is until it began to hail—"really big, about golf-ball size," she said. "So when it was over, we went outside, and all of our neighbors were outside looking at the hail and how crazy it was." When Kimberly and her mother went back into their home, the phone rang. "A neighbor gave us a call and said, 'Hey, look out your back window.' So we did." At the same time, her cellphone began to buzz, warning of imminent danger.

Before Kimberly and her mother returned to the basement, they looked out the back window once more. "We couldn't see anything...just a big green strip," she said. "About forty-five seconds after we got [downstairs], it hit. We both fell to the ground and stayed there. It felt like [it lasted] ten to fifteen seconds, then it was over. I wasn't very scared because I didn't believe it was happening.

"When it was all said and done, my mother looked up the basement steps and said, 'Oh, my God. We don't have a roof!' And I said, 'Don't be ridiculous. The windows just blew out.' I really didn't believe it until a few minutes later." Kimberly climbed the stairs and found nothing where there should have been two floors of the house. They had to climb over the rubble to get out to the street. The house, one of the first hit in Fairdale, was gone.

"We had heard glass and boards breaking in the wind—we definitely knew there were some broken things—but I thought we still had an upstairs," she said. "I don't really think it got scary until about fifteen or twenty minutes afterward, when we started hearing from all of the neighbors." And seeing the destruction. To Kimberly, it was "surreal...like being on the set of a movie," she said. "It didn't seem real. I've lived in this town my entire life, twenty-nine years at that point, and it was strange....It didn't look anything like it did forty minutes earlier."

A year later, their home and their lives are rebuilt. Kimberly joined hundreds of others—residents, first responders, volunteers, friends and well-wishers, as well as media and politicians—at an event on April 9, 2016, to remember what was lost and what never left. "It's nice to see smiles on my neighbors' faces, for sure," she said. "The toughest part? Seeing other people still hurting." Tears welled in her eyes at that. "Other than that, I think we've done a pretty good job of staying strong, staying positive."

Friends and next-door neighbors in life, Geraldine "Geri" Schultz and Jacklyn "Jackie" Klosa both perished in the tornado that leveled Fairdale.

Geri, sixty-seven, was described as a kindhearted and gentle woman who would go out of her way to help people. Geri and her husband, Clem, had just finished dinner when they heard on TV that a tornado was heading toward Davis Junction, a few miles to the west. "I was thinking [that] I sure hope it doesn't come this way," Clem said, "when [Geri] called me from the kitchen and said, 'Look out the window. It looks like a tornado coming up over the horizon.' I saw it and said, 'It sure does.'"

Clem headed to the second floor of the 175-year-old home to get lanterns in case the power went out and then looked out of a window and decided it was a good vantage point to watch for what was coming. "I could see it, and [I realized] I had my camera/phone," he said. After taking a picture, he turned on the phone's video function, thinking that the storm would turn west. It didn't. "I watched it walk right onto me," Clem said. "I rode the tornado down from the second floor."

The home Geri and Clem had turned from "a shack when we bought it…into a beautiful house" collapsed. "After the tornado, things got kind of quiet," Clem said. "I thought, 'Clem, are you dead?' And Clem said, 'No, you aren't dead, but you hurt. You can't hurt when you're dead.'"

Clem was able to dig his way out from under wood, plaster, boards and other debris to where he could see the sky and a face he didn't recognize. "But he knew my name," Clem said. The man helped Clem to his feet and sat him down on a beam. "He said, 'Sit here but don't look down.' I asked why, and he said, 'Your wife is right underneath you, and she's dead,'" Clem said. He found her body and checked for a pulse but found none. "There was nothing you could do," he said. Geri was in the kitchen when she died.

One of the last things Clem said he saw before the tornado struck was a framed studio photo of him and his wife, which disappeared in the storm. A few days after the tornado, that photo of Geri and her Clem appeared on Facebook. Clem's daughter, Sue Frazier, saw the photo in a post that read: "Found Items from the Fairdale Illinois Tornado." A woman had posted the photo after it was found in Harvard, about thirty-five miles northeast of Fairdale; it was returned to Clem.

While Geri Shultz was found right away, that wasn't what happened to her friend of fifteen years, Jackie Klosa. Jackie lived by herself in her Fairdale home, which was more than one hundred years old. That day, she never made it to the basement and sought refuge on the first floor of her home.

Yvette and Peter DeWispelaere were in Rockford getting their taxes done on April 9, 2015, when Yvette, Jackie's daughter, got two ominous signs. A friend in Tennessee sent a Facebook message wondering if they were OK. "They had heard about a tornado in Kirkland," she said. Yvette and Peter left, checking out the sky and noting that "it was kind of yucky," but heard no warnings on the car radio. Then a friend in Belvidere called her. "Are you OK?" the friend asked. "He said, 'Are you watching the news?' He said a tornado just hit Fairdale."

Yvette paused. Knowing that her mom lived in Fairdale, "it was like somebody punched me in the stomach," she said. She and her husband then made a quick stop at their home to grab reflective coats, water and flashlights; she jammed into her boots and was out of the house in less than a minute.

The drive from their Loves Park home is about twenty-five miles, and en route, she got a call from one of her mother's neighbors. "She said, 'The good news is that we're OK, but our house is gone. Jackie's house is gone, too, and they can't find Jackie.'"

Peter slammed on the brakes, but Yvette told him to keep on driving. She had a terrible feeling that something was very wrong.

When they came over the hill on Mulford Road, northwest of Fairdale, "all you could see was the red and blue glow from the emergency vehicles," she said.

"It was like the [lights] in *Field of Dreams*," Peter said. "It was just glowing."

The DeWispelaeres were forced to park near the intersection of Mulford Road and Route 72 because of downed power lines. When they got close to Fairdale, a sheriff's deputy recognized them and allowed them to enter what was left of the town. "The only thing on Mom's property was the roof to her garage, car, porch railing and a concrete slab," she said. "Her house was in a pile, about one story high. It had been a two-story house. We looked in the foundation, where I thought she would be. I said, 'If she's not in the basement, look for her bathtub.'"

After talking to authorities, they went to the holding station and stayed there until about 1:00 a.m., when they were told to go home because Jackie hadn't been found. The next day, the couple was notified that Jackie had been found where Yvette had told them to look: in her fiberglass bathtub. At about 10:00 a.m. on April 10, the couple returned to the site. "We parked at the driveway," she said. "I saw that the coroner had walked up the hill. The sheriff came out and said, 'We have some news…'

"The last year has been a roller coaster. There have been some real emotional days, some good memories. We got her taken care of, and that's all that matters." Yvette was glad to see so many turn out for the tornado memorial a year later. "This was wonderful," she said. "It was nice to visit with neighbors and friends."

As the Fairdale Tornado left the area, moving northeast, it lost speed and was downgraded to an EF1. But it still packed winds of eighty-five miles per hour when it plowed into the Summerfield Zoo on Flora Road south of Belvidere, which was preparing to open for the season. "We don't open until the end of April," said owner Rick Anderson, who was surprised at the impact of the storm. "We just thought it was a regular spring storm…[until] we went outside." What they saw prompted them to take shelter in the basement. "We couldn't see a tornado—I don't know if it was too close because it was so dark," Rick said.

After it hit, the zoo staff went out and saw a door in a tree and three of their buildings gone. Their greatest concern was the welfare of their animals. "There were animals lying around," Rick said. "Most of our fences were gone." The building that held the reindeer was gone, but the reindeer were safe. "We lost an emu and a black swan," he said. "That's terrible. But for what we have, it was pretty good."

Rick and his crew spent the first night corralling all of their loose animals. "It was no fun because it was dark and they were already scared," Rick said. Ponies, donkeys, reindeer and emu were out of their enclosures, but, Rick said, "they never actually left the property. We just didn't catch them right away. The ponies and donkeys were grazing like nothing had happened."

Rick asked his daughter to start a phone tree to get volunteers out to help, but others showed up on their own right away. "One person was driving by and stopped. There were storm chasers [who stopped] and said that they were going to help us."

Eventually, all the animals were accounted for, including an injured emu that was examined by the vet and given a thumbs up.

Even more people came out the next day. "Even before the sun came out, there were cars on the road," he said. "It was amazing. We had people come from different states and [some] who were here for a couple of weeks, just volunteering."

The zoo opened a couple weeks later, and since then, lost buildings have been replaced. In the storm's aftermath, they found a small miracle. "It was crazy," Rick said. "We had baby goats born during the tornado. The tornado hit the corner of the building, right by the baby goat house. It left that [corner] intact."

On April 9, 2016, hundreds of people gathered in Fairdale for the one-year anniversary of the tornado. Among those honored were first responders, volunteers, residents who helped and others. All were amazed at the recovery over the past twelve months, the rebuilding of homes and lives.

"The recovery is so remarkable," said Les Bellah, mayor of Kirkland, who coordinated emergency services and utilities, including Com Ed. "These people have got that midwestern 'get-it-done' attitude," he said.

Later in April 2015, Roger Miller, who farms eight hundred acres south of Interstate 90 and the Chrysler Assembly Plant off Town Hall Road in Belvidere, found something unusual on his land. Debris from the Fairdale Tornado had littered his property. "I had about eight pickup loads of debris that I hauled off," he said. "In the debris, I found a wedding dress, still on its hanger. It was beautiful with sequins on it, with no damage, but it was pretty muddy." He realized that somebody was missing a prized possession from a memorable day. "I couldn't hand it over in that condition," Roger said. "I took it to the cleaners, and he informed me that he didn't think he could clean it properly." David Perez of Neighborhood Cleaners in Belvidere told stateline.com, "When he showed it to me, I was unsure whether it could be cleaned and repaired." So he shipped it to an expert in New York.

Several months later, the dress was returned to Miller. In the meantime, the story about the found wedding dress was posted on Facebook, where Kelly Newman's son saw it. Kelly Newman's home was one of three destroyed by the tornado near the intersection of Routes 251 and 64. Kelly lost all of her belongings, including the wedding dress that she'd worn about four years earlier. "My son texted me and said, 'I think your dress is online,'" Kelly said. "So I went on there, and sure enough, there [it] was."

The reunion of Roger, Kelly and the dress took place at the dry cleaner. "She was real happy," Roger said. "It's beautiful!" Kelly said. "It looks just like brand-new."

It was a happy ending with one final twist. When Roger asked the specialty cleaner in New York for his bill, the cleaner said, "There's no charge."

Chapter 16

OTHER STORIES

This final chapter includes additional stories about the tornadoes that have struck Boone County. Some of the stories in this chapter appeared in the first tornado book. Others are stories that need to be told about the most recent tornadoes.

The First House Lost in 1967

The events of April 21, 1967, are clear to Rocky Rouse, even though he was only four years old. He remembers a stormy day with wicked hailstones. "They were golf ball sized, and my mom [Karen] gave me a Dixie cup, so I ran on the front porch and scooped some up," Rocky said. As the storm hit at 3:45 p.m., Rocky; his sister Laura, then nine; and his mother raced to the garage, where they rode out the storm in the knee hole of a desk. Their injuries were not serious: Laura got five stitches in her back, Rocky has a scar from a cut on his elbow and his mother had cuts and scrapes.

The home at 4700 Shropshire in Rockford was knocked down—roof gone, the main beam broken, walls collapsed. The *Rockford Morning Star* and the *Rockford Labor News* both reported that the damage was done by the Belvidere Tornado, but it probably wasn't. The home, located in southeast Rockford near the intersection of Samuelson Road and Twentieth Street, appears to be in line with the tornado's path, but the timing and location

An overhead shot of the activity at *Operation Belvidere*, a telethon that was broadcast on two Rockford TV stations and two radio stations on May 12, 1967. *Courtesy of Boone County Historical Museum.*

The late comedian Milton Berle (*left*) shakes hands with a local station representative at the Belvidere telethon, which raised more than $127,000. The June 14, 1967 edition of *Variety*, the famous show business daily newspaper, made note of its success. *Courtesy of Boone County Historical Museum.*

appear to make it a separate event. Roger Edwards of the National Weather Service said while it is "highly likely" the damage was the result of the same super cell, what occurred could have come from a tornado or "non-tornadic wind damage." But fifty years after the fact, nothing is certain.

Edwards said, "According to our records, which are quite prone to errors, the tornado started in the same county as Belvidere." And when the storm hit the Rouses' house at 3:45 p.m., the Belvidere Tornado may have been forming. Its first reported sighting came at 3:49 p.m. Clocks stopped at Belvidere High School at 3:50 p.m. "However, given the distance and *if* the damage in Rockford was with a tornado, either the Rockford time is wrong or the Belvidere Tornado start time is off," Edwards said.

One thing for certain is that Rocky's house was one of the first destroyed that day. "I remember that a bowl of Jell-O ended up on the front porch—still in the bowl," he said. "My mom was ironing [that afternoon], and the iron was still plugged in and on the ironing board. But the back wall was gone.

"To this day, nothing really scares me [except] when the wind blows, I get a little anxious."

The home was rebuilt on the site. "My dad [Walter] always chuckled at the carpenters, who said, 'Who builds a house with the shrubbery already there?'" Rocky said.

Suddenly, Shoes

Renee (Prell) McClenthen and her twin sister, Rhonda (Prell) Gunn, got a ride to their home on Glenwood Drive from Washington School on April 21, 1967. Although their parents, Ronald and Almyra, were at work, a family friend, Sally (Wold) Pitzrick, was staying with them. When the sky turned ominous, Sally insisted the ten-year-old fourth graders take shelter in the basement, where "[Sally] hovered over the top of us," Renee said. "I remember praying for God's care. Within moments, the house lifted slightly from the foundation, lifted again, and suddenly we could see daylight—every stick of wood, anything attached to the floor of the house, including the furnace and staircase, were completely gone."

Renee looked down and realized that she had not worn shoes when she went to the basement. "However, suddenly a *pair*—yes, not one but a pair—of boots landed in our basement for me to wear to protect my feet," she said.

"We then heard voices and men yelling down the basement asking if we were hurt. I don't know how, but they lifted the three of us [out]."

Their parents left their workplaces, desperate to find the twins. Almyra, who worked for the Belvidere school district, made it through the destruction to their house, only to find a hole in the ground and no children. Ronald, who had moved his family from Wisconsin the previous year for a job at the Chrysler Assembly Plant, went to the high school in hopes of locating his daughters. There he met his wife. A *Rockford Morning Star* photographer captured their anguished embrace in a photo that appeared in the April 22, 1967 edition. "The moment they were first reunited was published in papers all over the country," Renee said.

Renee recalled that as she and her sister made their way to the high school, they were "swept up by another family friend, Vern Pitzrick, who took us to a place of safety and then began to locate our parents, as well as those in need." Rhonda said that Vern "got out of the car, climbed a fence and headed to the [Chrysler] plant to find Dad. Sally, Renee and I were taken to a home to wait for our parents. Some hours later, our parents connected with Vern, and they arrived soaking wet and sobbing at finding us safe and sound."

For the next several weeks, the family stayed with friends while Ronald began to rebuild their house. "Father quickly constructed an apartment in the basement where we lived while he worked and rebuilt the house," Renee said. "[Living in the basement was] pretty crude" but manageable while the house was built.

"Our true hero is Sally Pitzrick, who still calls my mom on every anniversary of the tornado," said Rhonda. "God bless her for saving twin girls on April 21, 1967."

Yes, It Did Snow—But When?

"Then, it snowed the next day."

That is how many tornado survivors ended the stories they told about the Belvidere Tornado. The bizarre weather phenomena of the days from April 21 to 23, 1967, are forever embedded in their minds. That it was hot and humid on that Friday is indisputable.

It did snow—but not the next day, Saturday, April 22, as many people said. None of the Sunday, April 23, 1967 newspapers from Rockford,

Chicago or Milwaukee had pictures of snow, nor did they make mention of it. Pictures taken that day by professional photographer Harold Ryman show widespread damage—but no snow. There are many pictures that show snow falling or on the ground, including one of U.S. senator Charles Percy of Illinois talking to a recovery worker. So when were they taken?

The Monday, April 24 edition of the *Rockford Register-Republic* offers proof, under the headline "Yes, That White Stuff Is Snow." Following a record overnight low temperature of sixteen degrees, snow fell on Rockford and Belvidere on Sunday, April 23, 1967.

Belvidere Oasis Struck

The tornado of April 21, 1967, caused considerable damage at the Belvidere Oasis on the Jane Addams Memorial Tollway (Interstate 90), with shattered glass, toppled light standards and ruined items at the gift shop. Although the Oasis, located about a mile east of the Chrysler Assembly Plant, had about $20,000 in damage, none of the estimated two hundred people in the area at the time was injured.

Frank W. Boege, the executive director of the Illinois State Toll Highway Commission, arrived on the scene about an hour after the storm. He told the *Rockford Morning Star* that six large glass windows of the restaurant were blown in and another near the gift shop blew, damaging merchandise. Also, some food in cold storage was ruined.

At the two gas stations, one at each end of the rest stop, several vehicles were damaged by light standards that had toppled on them. One semi-truck was blown over, while several cars lost windows. Frank said, "Miraculously, there were no injuries because employees saw the tornado approaching and led everyone to the basement below the restaurant." Among the visitors were two buses of schoolchildren. The tollway authority responded immediately and dispatched crews to the rescue and recovery efforts in storm-ravaged Belvidere. Units from Hampshire, Park Ridge, Hinsdale and Rockford came to help, bringing more than one hundred maintenance workers. They reportedly worked until midnight, helping clear streets of debris.

Through Saturday, tollway police manned the Belvidere/Genoa Road exits off I-90, advising motorists to stay clear of the area and rerouting them. Power was out at the Oasis for about four days after the storm.

Short Stories

- April 21, 1967, was such a nice day that Linda Jarvis did something she never did before or after: she skipped school. She simply walked out of Belvidere High School and went home. Because it was such a nice day, she decided to get some sun. "I went upstairs and laid out on the roof," Linda said. "That's what I liked to do." Because she took shelter at home, she wasn't at the high school, where her frantic mother was searching for her. They eventually were reunited.
- Belvidere mayor Clair Hetland tried to beat the storm and get home to close the garage door and check for any open windows. But just as he pulled into his driveway on Highland Street, the tornado hit. "I fell down on the floor of the car," he told the *Rockford Register-Republic*. "The wind picked up the car and set it down several times and I lay there as the debris piled up." A second family car was picked up from the driveway and hurled into the home with such force that it was wedged halfway into a bedroom wall. The house was demolished. "Our house is gone, but we're all right," the mayor's wife said. While his house was destroyed, he found that four closets were virtually untouched, and he was able to find "a dry pair of shoes."
- Anita Thies was shopping with her sons Kevin, four, and Kerry, one, when the tornado struck. Unable to get to their home on East Avenue, she took her sons to her parents' farm. Anita's husband, Orin, found much damage to their home, but his pickup truck was drivable. As Orin made his way north on East Avenue, he spotted Anita and her father tromping through knee-deep mud. "We collapsed into each other's arms," said Anita, who added, "Where's Princess?" Their six-year-old beagle was nowhere to be found. They searched for her for days, leaving food behind at their home in case she returned. On May 12, exactly three weeks after the storm, the family received a phone call from a repairman at their home. "This guy calls and says there's a beagle here who's whining and crying," Orin said. "We went over, and there she was." Weak and thin after her three-week ordeal, Princess had suffered "a nervous breakdown and a tumor that the vet said came out because of the stress," Anita said. "But she came out fine. She lived until she was fifteen."
- And you thought it only happened in movies. Bus driver Jack Frint told the students on his bus to open the windows and get under the

seats just before the tornado struck. Helen Dean Poirier did that but poked her head up to get a look—and "saw a cow fly by." A flying cow was a special effects marvel in the 1996 film *Twister*.

- When a reporter for the *Milwaukee Journal* researched his story at the Community Building, where the Red Cross had its emergency headquarters, he found these items that had been brought there: a rain-soaked composition notebook with only the name Kristine, nineteen pairs of muddy shoes with their laces still tied, a boy's red hat with a partially chewed chin strap, a girl's mud-caked satchel and many small coats and jackets.
- One of the most ironic stories uncovered during research for the original tornado book was one that appeared in the *Belvidere Daily Republican*. It told how Belvidere's two hospitals, St. Joseph's and Highland, had contracted with a federal public health service, through the Illinois Department of Public Health, to provide supplies in the event of a disaster. St. Joseph's was to be the site of a Packaged Disaster Hospital, which would provide adequate medical equipment and supplies, cots and bedding and pharmaceuticals to set up a two-hundred-bed hospital. The value of the equipment was $45,000. The material to supply each hospital was expected to arrive within six to nine weeks. The story, with the headline "Hospitals to Receive Disaster Equipment," appeared on April 20, 1967—one day before the tornado.
- On May 12–13, 1967, *Operation Belvidere*, a telethon, was held and broadcast on WREX-TV (channel 13), WCEE-TV (channel 23), WROK-AM and WRRR-AM. The event raised more than $127,000, and its success was mentioned in the June 14, 1967 edition of *Variety*, the famous show business daily newspaper. Also, the city of Belvedere, California, held a "Belvedere to Belvidere" tornado relief drive through the American Red Cross.
- The commencement exercises for Belvidere High School's class of 1967 were scheduled to be held in the gym of the new building. But because of damage, the event was held in the Community Building, site of previous graduations. Many graduates were disappointed because of this.

The Greenhouse Was a Safe House

An overlooked Belvidere landmark destroyed by the tornado was Sunnyside Greenhouse, once located on East Avenue, north of the high school. The building was pretty much leveled, but the business provided a tremendous service that day, helping to save lives in many ways.

Just prior to the storm, owner Henry Strawn, his wife, seven of his workers and a group of children ran to safety in a storm shelter the owner had the foresight to build under the greenhouse. "My wife saw [the storm] coming and she pulled a bunch of school kids off the street and we took them into the basement," Strawn told the *Rockford Morning Star*. "It was dark down there and I grabbed a youngster. I said, 'Who have I got?' The youngster replied, 'You've got me.' I didn't know who that was, but it didn't make any difference."

Strawn's wife continued to help others. "She did a wonderful job," Marion Anderson, a worker, said. "She went out and got some more kids and pulled them into the front of the building. She pushed the children

The Fox Skating Rink, located across the street from Immanuel Lutheran School, was demolished. *Courtesy of Boone County Historical Museum.*

While adults rummage through what is left of a home, a girl looks to the future. *Courtesy Boone County Historical Museum.*

under a counter just as the tornado blew out the plate glass windows. None of them was hurt and none of us."

After Henry brought some injured students to the high school, he turned his damaged delivery truck into a makeshift ambulance. Leslie

(Knott) Lindsey and her brother Rick Knott, both injured on a bus, recalled how they were taken to St. Joseph's Hospital in a florist's van. "I remember it was damaged and didn't have any windows," Leslie said. "We got into a white van from Sunnyside," Rick said. "I remember driving over trees and around trees and poles."

Two Stories—Two Last-Second Decisions

Dave Englund was sitting in the front seat of a friend's car; four others were sitting in the back. The friend's mother was going to drive them home on April 21, 1967. They were in a car that was parked on Circle Drive when the storm approached. "I saw five funnel clouds coming straight at us," he said. "In a split second, we had to decide if we were better off in the car or running." They stayed in the car, but Dave was disoriented. He doesn't remember what happened, but he was later told that at the moment the tornado hit, the driver reached over, grabbed his collar and flipped him into the back seat. "At that moment, the steering wheel collapsed [on the friend's mother] and broke her sternum. I don't know if she would have been killed had she stayed in that normal position," he said. The car flew twenty-five feet, with all inside safe. "The girl in the car crawled out of the back, and we all crawled out on our stomachs."

Like Dave and the driver who pulled him to safety, six-year-old Scott Schwebke and his mother, Verna Schwebke, were not wearing seat belts, which was common fifty years ago. Verna was driving south on East Avenue across from the high school with Scott in the middle of the back seat when she spotted the tornado. "She immediately pulled over to her right into someone's driveway," said Scott, who was craning his neck trying to see the funnel cloud. "I said, 'I don't see it,'" Scott said, and at that moment, the car stopped and his mother reached over the front seat and pulled him to the front and threw him under the dashboard. "She laid on top of me. I still…I can remember the car just bouncing. It didn't move, but it went up and down, up and down, up and down."

All the windows of the car were gone, and during the storm, his mother had been pummeled with debris. "Her hair, her back and neck were full of glass," he said. "It penetrated her skin." An aunt who was a nurse removed all the debris from her, Scott said. He knows his mother acted instinctively to protect him. "Oh, she saved my life," he said. "I don't think there's any doubt. I would have been torn to shreds."

They Were Left for Dead

Bruce Poirier was getting ready for baseball practice when Coach Joe Lewis directed the players to the southwest corner of the Belvidere High School gym. There, they watched the roof beam "flex up and down about a foot," Bruce said. They ran for safety, but he returned to the gym, which became an emergency morgue. "I grabbed the keys to the first-aid room and got supplies, then ran out to the coach's car, where another first-aid kit was," he said. Bruce said he helped set up the morgue, getting pads, cots and divider walls. Then he went outside to help survivors, first to a bus where he found one of his friends trapped underneath. "We took him to the morgue because they thought he was dead," Bruce said. "But he came to. He wasn't dead. He staggered up, knocked down one of the walls and everyone started screaming."

Robert Ellison's bus driver tried to grab him and pull him into the bus as the twister approached, but Robert broke away in an attempt to run to the high school. He grabbed another student, Joellen Roan, and said, "Joellen, we're going to die!" Robert saw the bus rolling toward him. "I turned around, and the bus rolled over me," he said. "I was left for dead. [But] when they came to pronounce me dead, I had a little heartbeat."

Robert had head lacerations requiring two hundred stiches, a broken pelvis and fractured ribs. He was in such grave condition that his situation was made public. "They broadcast names, and someone told my parents to get to the hospital [because] it was life or death for me. By the grace of God, I survived." He was hospitalized for three weeks at St. Anthony and said years later that when he was there, a nurse recognized him and told him that his ear was attached only by tendons and gristle.

While hospitalized, Robert made the news when he received a letter from President Lyndon Johnson. In a *Rockford Register-Republic* story, his parents were at a loss why he received a letter on White House stationery until they opened the envelope. It read:

> *Dear Bobby,*
> *When President Johnson learned about you from your cousin, Barbara Dahlstedt (age 13 of Phoenix, Arizona), she asked me to write this note. The President is indeed sorry you suffered injury, but he trusts that by this time you are feeling much better. He sends you every good wish.*
> *Sincerely, Juanita Roberts, personal secretary to the President.*

He Was a Hero, Whoever He Was

John Gallano isn't sure who the man was, but he will always be a hero. John, a freshman at BHS, was at the south end of the school, waiting for the bus with some of his friends. They were stunned by what they saw. "We actually saw the tornado approach," John said. "We didn't know what to make of it. Thankfully, some older people got our attention and started gathering everybody up and herded us into the high school. I was one of the last to go in."

When John watched the roof of Highland Hospital go skyward, he realized how grave the situation was. As one of the last to enter the school, he saw a teacher bolt to the door. "My last recollection just before the tornado hit was Mike Morris leaving the safety of the building," he said. "He saw a young girl on the south side of the school, and she started to be caught up in the wind and debris.

"This guy ran about thirty feet outside the building, grabbed her and rushed back in. It couldn't have been more than a second or two after that that the tornado caught up to the building and took out all of the glass in that section. I'm convinced that this guy saved that girl's life. She had become disoriented and couldn't see how to get into the building. I can't say with 100 percent certainty that it was Mike Morris. But I am 95 percent sure."

"One of Those Miracles"

All three children in the Knott family of Garden Prairie were on buses that day—buses that went rolling in the wake of the Belvidere Tornado. The eldest, Leslie, a junior at Belvidere High School, was on a bus that was about sixth in line. Her brothers—Doug, an eighth grader, and Rick, a seventh grader—both attended Belvidere Junior High; they were on another bus. Their mother, Ruth Knott Ross, remembered getting a call from her husband, who asked if everything was all right. He informed her about the tornado, and she said she realized right away that something was wrong.

The driver of Leslie's bus told the students to get down. But Leslie was curious. "Of course, I didn't want to get down," she said. "I wanted to see a tornado. I had never seen one. [Then] one of the guys on the bus threw himself on top of me [and] said, 'You've got to get down, Leslie.'" She did but looked up to see the windows cracking and the bus rocking. When it was over, she left the bus with one thought: "Where are my brothers?"

Rick recalled that driver Gilbert Julin ordered the students to get in their seats with their heads down. Then the wind started to blow and hail began to pelt the bus. "The next thing was that the bus started to roll over and over," Rick said. "It was almost like being in space; the bus was rotating on us. It was weird." Rick said he was knocked out for a time, and when he came to his senses, he thought the bus was empty. "I remember looking around and seeing someone in the back," he said. "It was another kid from Garden Prairie, so I pulled him out. We went out through the front window and down the hood. The bus was sitting so low, it had sunk into the ground, which was soft and muddy. When we came around the side of the bus, heading toward the school, we saw somebody put a towel over a person who had gone through a window and ended up under the bus."

Looking for his brother, Rick went into the school, where he was reunited with his sister. Both were taken to St. Joseph's Hospital, where their parents found them. "They asked if we were all right," Leslie said. "We said we were OK. We got up to give them a big hug, and when Rick stood up, they saw blood where he had been sitting." Rick had a broken collarbone, a puncture in the back of his leg and a broken wrist. Leslie broke her clavicle and had cuts and bruises. When the two found their parents, they said, "We can't find Doug." They had been looking for him everywhere.

What Rick didn't know was that Doug was still on the bus when he scooted out the window and down the hood. When Doug was rescued, no one could identify him. Because he had a serious brain stem injury, he was taken to St. Anthony Hospital. There, a neighbor identified him and gave the medical staff permission to perform surgery to relieve the pressure on his brain, which had swelled. When the Knotts got to St. Anthony about midnight, they were hit with grim news. "They really didn't give him much chance to make it," Ruth said. The next day was Doug's birthday, and Ruth said the hospital called to tell them that the prognosis was dim. After surgery, Doug went into a coma.

He was still in a coma some weeks later when Ruth called on a different source. "We stopped at our minister's house and said a prayer," she said. While they were praying, Doug came out of his coma. "It was one of those miracles," Ruth said. Even his doctor was surprised. "His recovery was amazing. His specialist went away for a few days, and when he came back,

Doug was able to walk to him," she said. "The doctor said [that] any more instances like this, and he was going into the ministry."

Doug underwent months of therapy, overcoming fears that he would be severely disabled. "It probably took a year to get him back to where he had been before the tornado," Rick said. After high school, Doug followed his father's path and joined the U.S. Marines. He was working at the Chrysler Assembly Plant in 1979 when he died. He was twenty-six. "Maybe he was on borrowed time," Rick said.

Three Stories from the South Side

Most Belvidere High School students who lived south of the school boarded buses on the south side, several hundred feet away from where the twister struck the school on the north side.

As usual, Diane (Anderson) Onley had been dropped off from the bus that had taken her from Immanuel Lutheran School to the transfer point on the north side and then walked through the school to the south to catch her bus home. The tornado struck just as she got on the bus, where she rode it out. Once it passed, she joined others running back to the school. "I walked—or should I say ran—right out of my shoes!" she said. "I had loafers on, and they were all stuck in the mud. In the school, everybody was crying and scared. I was with my older sister, and when we got into the school, I was going to take a Kleenex out of my purse—and there was nothing in it. [Everything] was sucked out of my purse."

Cheryl (Fowler) Sturges was in a grassy area, waiting for her bus, when the driver yelled for them to get back into the school. She was directed to the cafeteria, where she and others ducked under tables. As they lay there, they could hear glass breaking, children screaming and terrifying sounds. "It was just like they say….It sounds like a train," she said. "There was such a roar. I didn't know if the roof was coming off the building." When she realized her two siblings were on the bus she was waiting for, she dashed back outside to find them. Pelted with hail, they were forced to go back into the building, where she was directed to the north side of the building. "Everybody was bringing in people on doors, and you could hardly tell who they were from all of the mud and tar on them," Cheryl said. "Teachers, some of them crying, were trying to help bring those kids in. I found my little brother [Craig, eight] and my sister [Connie, ten].

They were safe. We were very fortunate." They were on their bus when the driver, sensing trouble, told the riders to get under their seats. "When you see pictures or saw the real thing and saw those buses on the north side that were flipped and rolled and everything else…and for [Craig and Connie's bus] to roll into a ditch and wedge itself against a power pole…" she said, unable to complete her thought.

Nancy Johnson was on a bus that had gotten a warning from police captain "Dutch" Whalen about the approaching storm. Before it could move, a girl ran off the bus and started to cry for her mother. "The bus driver slapped her and made her get back into the bus," said Nancy, a fourth grader. The bus was about halfway between the high school and old Route 5 (U.S. 20) when the tornado hit, which put it at the southern edge of the storm. After it passed, they all went to the library, where Nancy recalled that someone asked them, "Are you ready to see God?"

Caledonia Hit Hard

With a population of just under two hundred, Caledonia has had its share of tornado tragedy. An EF2 tornado that destroyed several homes in November 2010 left no deaths or injuries, but the community was hard hit in the 1967 Belvidere Tornado, when seven of the seventeen students killed were residents—all on the same bus. Those killed were Kent Ferguson, twelve; Pamela Haines, fourteen; Bruce Lindley, thirteen; Theodore "Ted" Nelson, fifteen; Dwight David Shaw, eleven; Timothy Smith, seventeen; and Phyllis Van Brocklin, thirteen.

Sue (Walter) Holmes, a first grader at Caledonia School, recalled the events that began with rain, wind and hail. After dropping off a station wagon load of schoolchildren to their home, her mother and Sue got home to find there was no electricity. "At that point, I decided I should be scared," Sue said. "We had a big weather radio, and we turned it on, and it seemed the first thing they said was that a tornado had hit Belvidere High School. I looked and saw my mom start to cry." Then the phone rang. "It was one of the daughters of my mom's dear friend Marilyn Orr, who said her grandma [Norine Wych] had a heart attack watching the storm, and would my mom please come over."

Uncharacteristically, her mother left Sue and her siblings, then seven and two, home. "My mother never left us home," Sue said. Soon, Sue's father got home with her older brother Greg, who had been at the high school. "He looked shell-shocked and was just filthy," she said. Her brother left his bus and "didn't remember a thing until a girl pulled him out of the mud and took him inside to wash him up to figure out who he was.

"The TV was on, and the only thing they were showing was a list of people who were missing. There were names that were familiar to us," Sue said.

Then the phone calls started coming. "Our next-door neighbor had three kids in high school," Sue said. "Tim Smith, who ended up dying from his injuries. Ann Smith had two broken legs from a bus landing on her. She was in a wheelchair for weeks. At some point, Jack Lindley called to say, 'I can't find my son. Please come and help me find my son.' So Dad went to help, and they did find him, and he was killed. Bruce Lindley was his name."

More calls came to their house with news about Caledonia students. One girl had severe internal injuries, while her brother broke his shoulder. Two more boys were severely injured. "And then the call came in that they found Teddy Nelson, and he was killed."

That night, Sue's brother Greg found he couldn't pick up his legs to get into bed, so his parents examined him and found "he had a dimple [on his back], not a wound," said Sue. Her father got in touch with a doctor, who said to open it with a sterile blade and see if there was something in there. "They did that and pulled out two pieces of wood, which must have been pushing onto his spine somewhere," she said. "He still carries the two pieces with him."

Hero without a License

Gary Loofboro was on a bus that left Belvidere High School before the tornado struck and was home when his father, a part-time Boone County deputy sheriff, got a call to report to the high school. Gary asked if he could come along. He made it to the high school, where he was standing near the entrance and ran into Randall Trueblood, an acquaintance who was desperately looking for his daughter. Randall had driven his station wagon to the school and was asked to transport a little boy to the hospital. Looking for help, he saw Gary. "I said, 'Gary, come with me,' so he got into the wagon and we went to St. Joseph's Hospital," Randall said.

Upon arrival, they were told the hospital couldn't handle the boy and were asked to take him to Rockford. "Knowing that I had not found my daughter, I said, 'I can't go. I've gotta stay here,'" Randall said. "So I asked [Gary], 'Can you drive?' He said yes but that he didn't have his license. I said, 'You take him to Rockford anyway,' and away he went."

Gary said, "I was scared to death. My dad was a policeman, and all of that was on my mind." Not only that, he wound up driving to all three hospitals in Rockford. "First we went to St. Anthony, and they said they were full," he said. "Then we tried to go to [Swedish-American], which was also full. Then they told me to go to Rockford Memorial, and I had no idea where that was. I remember stopping at gas stations and asking how to get there. Somehow we got to Rockford Memorial.

"Then I drove the car back to Belvidere. It was wild. I didn't tell my dad about it until it was all over."

The Famous Photo

Curtis N. Kitchen was wet and standing in mud, trying to protect his camera. The *Rockford Morning Star* photographer had positioned himself so that the storm-scattered letters that once spelled out "Belvidere High School" were in the background of a picture. In the foreground, nine tornado victims, soaked and dirty, began to walk toward him. "I waited for just the right moment....I wanted them in front of that sign. Water was cascading off of my camera," Kitchen said in the June 1967 edition of the *Gannetteer*, a publication for employees of the Gannett Group, which then owned the two Rockford newspapers. "I was soaked to the skin. I took two quick shots, moving with the people and the wind, and I knew the picture had a lot of feeling. Actually none of the survivors knew anyone had photographed them. And I didn't realize the full impact of what I had done until my film was developed and the prints were made."

After taking several shots, he got the most famous photo of the Belvidere Tornado and one of the most well-known disaster photos ever taken. For several years, it appeared in *World Book Encyclopedia* in its tornado section. The image appears on one of the murals in downtown Belvidere.

In the picture are siblings Kathy (Fitch) Loy, then fifteen, and her brother John Fitch, eighteen; Harry Wennmacher, thirty-eight; his wife, Ann, thirty-five; their son Paul, five; his daughters Donna, fifteen, and Linda, fourteen;

Curtis N. Kitchen took the most famous photo of the tornado, showing survivors and family members heading into the elements that followed the tornado. *Rockford Morning Star.*

Judy Hage, fifteen; and Connie Jeanblanc, thirteen. "We were in the library when they announced that they had [vehicles] out front for us," Kathy Fitch said. "So a group of us walked out the corridor to the front door. That's when he took the picture."

"I wasn't immediately aware of the dramatic interest of the tornado victims' facial expressions," Kitchen said.

"That picture went all over the country," John Fitch said. "In a day or two, after everybody had seen the picture, it was pretty neat."

But the nine found out that being part of history has its downside as well. To this day, when news accounts appear with the famous photo, Kathy said, "I get people telling me that I saw your picture." For those in the picture, having to recall the pain of that day was a struggle; they also did not appreciate being viewed as the "faces" of the tornado.

Back to School

Students at Immanuel Lutheran School returned to classes a week after the storm—but not in the damaged building. School was held at the church's former location on Boone Street and at Evangelical Covenant Church. "Thanks to an outpouring of gifts from people near and far, Immanuel Lutheran School was rebuilt and ready for occupancy the next school year," Pastor Eugene Wille said. "One can imagine the joy and thanksgiving of our church family at this rededication of our school. This time it was our songs of praise that raised the gym roof, not the tornado."

Belvidere's public schools, other than Belvidere High School, reopened on Wednesday, April 26, without bus service or school lunches. Most of the district's food supply was used during rescue operations. Repairs to the high school began the week after the tornado. The most damage was to the roof and ventilators, and most of the building's glass was blown out. Aside from mud and water, classrooms were in good shape.

BHS reopened on Monday, May 1, with about one hundred absences. The normal absence rate was seventy-five. Leslie (Knott) Lindsey, who broke her clavicle on a bus, recalling that first day back said, "It was like the walking wounded. Everybody was on crutches or had bad cuts and scars." Principal Virgil McAllister said in a newspaper account that students could claim purses and other lost items at the Community Building. He also noted, sadly, that all records of grades had been recovered.

Providing Comfort Where Needed

Shortly after the deadly Fairdale Tornado in April 2015, Immanuel Lutheran Church in Belvidere got a call to provide a special kind of help. The church is affiliated with the Canine Comfort Dog Ministry of Lutheran Church Charities. Fairdale had just begun to recover when two golden retrievers, Kye and Bekah, were summoned to the devastated community. "Usually when a tragedy happens, the dogs are called out," said Sue Piske, the person in charge of the comfort dogs program at the church. "We were in there right afterward. The roads were still pretty messed up, and they weren't letting anybody in. But they did let the comfort dogs in. So a lot of families who were just heartbroken with all that had happened to them were able to enjoy a little visit from the dogs and get comfort. [People] flocked to them."

The dogs from Immanuel Lutheran were among other comfort dogs brought to Fairdale. "Two of our team members brought them in," Piske said. "We have a team of seventeen handlers. The handlers go through training, and the dogs are trained about a year in order to get into the program. They are trained from six weeks old."

The contingent continued the comfort program long after the initial response. "We went back several times," Sue said. "We were part of a group that went there for months afterward."

Comfort dogs and grief counselors were not part of the picture fifty years ago. Former BHS assistant principal Joan Brannah recalled that there were "a couple of counselors" on hand when the high school reopened on April 27, 1967; six days after the disaster, there were no other people on hand to help guide students. Dennis Norem, an eighth grade student then but a doctor today, said that "in that day, there were no counselors. Most people that had been in the tornado didn't want to talk about it because you had friends killed, and there was a lot of anger.

"Our parents really didn't encourage us because nobody knew how to deal with those kinds of things. You just went back to school, and you said, 'OK, that was that, and it's time to move on.'"

INDEX

A

Anderson, Gregory 128
Anderson, John B. 47
Anderson, Marion 171
Anderson, Rick 162
Ardenfeld, Howard 110

B

Bailey, Deanna 52
Bangert, Carl 30
Barr, Jim 66, 80, 81
Bates, Michael 133, 139
Bellah, Les 163
Bell, John 67, 68
Bentley, Lonna 12
Benzel, Lorene 61
Benzel, Ollie 76
Berle, Milton 165
Beu, Phil 88
Biggins, Mrs. 70
Blum, LeRoy 41, 43, 44
Boege, Frank W. 168
Bowley, Ken 58
Boyd, Kathleen J. 23, 75
Brannah, Joan 85, 183
Brenner, Betty 48
Brereton, Fred 79
Brooks, Mabel 35, 36
Bryan, Kraig 133, 134
Bryan, Kurt 133, 134

C

Carlson, Debbie 50
Carlson, Melinda 63
Carlson, Ron 51
Carlson, Shirley 50, 51
Casey, Sheri 31
Chance, Steven 134
Chilson, Donna 147
Church, John 69, 71
Collins, Martha 89
Cordray, Buck 130
Cordray, Jim 130
Cordray, Pop 130
Craig, Shirley (Turner) 44
Crawford, A.J. 147
Cregeen, Sandra 142
Cross, Karen 110, 131

D

Dahlstedt, Barbara 175
Dal Pra, Jerry 30
Dal Pra, Tony 30, 31
Damm, Pam (Wilson) 131
Dannenberg, Mrs. Harry 127
Darmon, Johnny 71
Day, Cindy 139, 150
Day, Mary Lou 139
Day, Ronald 139
Day, Ruth 140
Decker, Barbara Jo 140
Decker, Lawrence 44, 140, 150
Decker, Lloyd 140
Decker, Lori Ann 140
Decker, Marcella 140
Decker, Terry 140
Denning, Bill 49
Dettmann, Dr. 36, 37
DeWane, Ray 93, 94, 110
DeWispelaere, Peter 161
DeWispelaere, Yvette 161, 162
Duclon, Norma 112, 144
Dye, Ivan 134

E

Eakin, Cecelia 140
Eby, Lowell 129
Edwards, Bernard 128
Edwards, Betty 153
Edwards, Bob 153
Edwards, Roger 25, 26, 166
Elliot, Randy 58
Ellis, Dr. Jim 98
Ellison, Robert 175
Englund, Dave 173
Erickson, Susan 146

F

Fadden, Michael 31
Farina, Jean 110
Faris, Harry 58
Ferguson, Becky Lynn 140
Ferguson, Ken 54
Ferguson, Kent 140, 179
Ferguson, Martha 140
Ferguson, Mrs. Wilbur 140
Ferguson, Nadeen 140
Ferguson, Scott 140
Ferguson, Shirley 53, 54
Ferguson, Wilbur 140
Fisher, Donald 109, 110
Fisher, Douglas Eugene 110
Fitch, John 181
Fitch, Walter 51
Ford, Judi 75
Fossati, Grace 119
Fowler, Cindy 83
Fowler, Connie 83
Fowler, Craig 83
Frank, Rick 27
Frazier, Sue 160
Frint, Jack 169
Fritz, Ed 51
Funnsinn, Beth (Dulgar) 104

G

Gallano, John 175
Gentille, Lieutenant William 124
Gorham, Doug 79
Gorham, Ralph 105
Gray, Sandra (Mallett) 135
Grayson, Cheryl (Ferguson) 53
Greves, Ed 98
Grout, E. Dean 120
Guerke, Arnold 86
Gunn, Rhonda (Prell) 166
Gustafson, Donald 140
Gustafson, Harold 93, 140
Gustafson, Minnie 140

H

Hage, Judy 181
Haines, Kimberly 141
Haines, Pam 72, 137, 141, 179
Haines, Stanley 137, 141
Haines, Virginia 137, 141

Hajek, Alice 58, 61
Hall, Barb 153, 154
Hall, Ken 153, 154
Halverson, Orrie 81
Hammond, Barbara 90, 92, 125, 126
Hammond, Bill 90, 92, 125, 126
Hamre, Mary 94
Hamre, Mary Jean 141
Harned, Charlie 84
Harris, Elizabeth 134
Harvey, James 93
Hawkey, Esther 35, 37, 121
Hernandez Eloy, Connie 158
Hetland, Clair 118, 125, 126, 169
Hicks, Sherry (Page) 63, 65
Hinrichs, Marge 82, 84
Holmes, Sue (Walter) 179
Hurley, Aneita Ann 68, 81
Hyser, Craig 141

J

Jarvis, Linda 169
Jeanblanc, Connie 181
Jennings, John 18
Johnson, Barbara 116, 141
Johnson, Donald 141
Johnson, Donald, Jr. 141
Johnson, Gerald 141
Johnson, Glenn 37
Johnson, Hugh H. 136
Johnson, Martin 66, 67
Johnson, Maxine 141
Johnson, Nancy 178
Johnson, Thad 39
Johnson, William 66, 81
Juhlin, Bruce 141
Julin, Gilbert 45, 72, 142, 176
Jury, Jason, Sr. 106, 108

K

Kaiser, Barbara Ann 105, 116
Kaiser, Mary 105
Kastning, Chuck 154
Keegan, Eugene "Jinx" 124
Keegan, Teri (Turner) 72, 142
Kerner, Otto 39, 128
Kibby, Glenn 67
Kiefer, Ruth 30
Kitchen, Curtis N. 181
Klosa, Jacklyn "Jackie" 158, 160, 161
Knott, Rick 173, 176, 177
Knutson, Jan (Fiebranz) 34, 37, 39
Kudzma, Bernie 119

L

LaBuy, Arty 66, 67
Lamping, Judy (Gorham) 53
Lantz, Jim 64, 65, 118
Lawrence, Harlan 144
Lehman, Linda (Trueblood) 66, 114
Lewis, Joe 79, 174
Lindley, Bruce 70, 143, 144, 179, 180
Lindley, Doug 143
Lindley, Jack 143, 180
Lindley, Judy 143
Lindley Lepp, Adah Maurine 143
Lindley, Pamela 143
Lindsey, Leslie (Knott) 173, 182
Loofboro, Gary 180
Loy, Kathy (Fitch) 181
Luke, Sister Mary 117, 118, 121
Lutz, Malvina (Hart) 15, 55, 65, 66, 80, 82, 85
Lutzow, Cristine 51, 144
Lutzow, Donna 144
Lutzow, Everett 144
Lutzow, Harlan 144
Lutzow, Lawrence 144
Lutzow, Mrs. Everett 144
Lyford, Linda (Ohlsen) 53

M

Maars, Jerry 130
Mallett, Dan 135
Mangiaracina, Kathleen 119
Manley, Rick 44
Marander, W.C. "Bill" 18
Martin, Lorraine 62

Mason, Terry 51
Matheson, Celestia 74
McAllister, Virgil 84, 85, 86, 182
McCain, Joyce 147
McClain, Sandra 31
McClenthen, Renee (Prell) 166
McGhee, Thomas 89
McHugh, Ellen 121
McLain, Robert 144
McLain, Sandra 144
Miles, Ethel 35, 37
Miller, Roger 129, 163
Morgan, Ralph 118, 125
Morris, Gary 58
Morris, Mike 176

N

Nelson, Cathy 79
Nelson, LaVern 145
Nelson, Lawrence “Larry” 145
Nelson, Margaret 144
Nelson, Theodore “Ted” 144, 147, 179, 180
Newman, Kelly 163
Norem, Dennis 69, 70, 141, 149, 183

O

O’Donnell, Eleanor 32, 120
O’Mallcy, Eugene 118
Onley, Diane (Anderson) 15, 178
Orr, Marilyn 150, 179

P

Paulson, Ken 123
Pavlak, Sally (Ferguson) 53
Pearson, Harriet 31
Pederson, Tom 69
Percy, Charles 124, 168
Perez, David 163
Peters, Myrtle 150
Piske, Sue 183
Pitzrick, Sally (Wold) 166, 167
Pitzrick, Vern 167
Pivoras, Anna 9
Poe, David Wayne 146, 150
Poe, Mrs. Wayne 146
Poe, Wayne 146
Poirier, Bruce 174
Poirier, Helen Dean 170
Pond, Don 58
Popp, Greg 51
Powell, Shirley 120
Powers, Tom 67
Prather, Marty 68, 73, 127
Pratt, Molly 115
Pulliam, Don 128

R

Radostits, Kimberly 158
Rauner, Bruce 157
Reed, Randolph 142
Reeser, Nina 37
Rehn, Dorothy 140
Reininger, Kelly 154
Roan, Joellen 175
Roberts, Juanita 175
Ross, Ruth Knott 176
Rouse, Rocky 164
Rowe, Jerry 8
Ryman, Harold 168
Ryman, Marjorie 49
Ryman, Ron 49

S

Schmidt, Maynard 128
Schultz, Clem 160
Schultz, Geraldine “Geri” 158, 160
Schultz, Naomi 87
Schultz, Sandra 147
Schumacher, Joel 86, 89
Schuster, Marvin 68
Schwebke, Scott 174
Schwebke, Verna 174
Shattuck, Debbie 102
Shattuck, Diane 102
Shaw, Dennis 146
Shaw, Dwight David 146, 179
Shaw, Dwight Leslie 146

Shaw, Jean 146
Shaw, Lester 146
Shaw, Tammy 146
Shepherd, Jim 26, 27, 28
Shue, Linda 84
Small, Penny (Pearse) 74
Smiley, Roy 100
Smith, Ann 179
Smith, Bonnie 105
Smith, Dr. 36, 37
Smith, Elizabeth 150
Smith, Genela 147
Smith, Jim 147
Smith, Timothy 146, 179
Smith, Vicky Jo 147
Smith, Willie 147
Steinke, Kay 20
Steinke, Larry 23, 75
Steinke, Steve 15, 19
Stephenson, Tammy 71
Stoll, Jack 19, 31, 147
Strathman, Elmer 93
Strawn, Henry 171
Sturges, Cheryl 83, 178
Swanson, Mrs. Rodney 127

T

Tate, Carol 147
Tate, Evelyn 147
Tate, John 147
Tate, Johnnie 147, 148
Tate, Judy 147
Taylor, Tom 67
Thies, Anita 169
Thomas, Dick 101, 130
Thornton, Bonnie Nelson 66
Thustad, Lois 146
Trueblood, Peggy 106
Trueblood, Randall 115, 180
Turner, Ann 95, 98, 129
Turner, Gary 95, 128, 129
Turner, Jim 99, 101, 128, 130
Turner, Lloyd 95, 97, 98, 99

V

Van Brocklin, Mary 149
Van Brocklin, Orville 149
Van Brocklin, Phyllis 72, 149, 179
Vogelsang, Alma 149
Vogelsang, Becky 89, 149
Vogelsang, Clarence 149

W

Walker, John 68
Walraven, Rick 155
Walters, Dennis 49
Warner, Joel 58
Wearmouth, Roxanne 72
Wennmacher, Harry 94, 181
Whalen, Francis "Dutch" 57, 58, 64, 68, 111, 178
Wheeler, Roger 76, 79, 83
Wheeler, Russ 27
White, Mary Ann 45
Wille, Eugene 86, 87, 88, 89, 149, 182
Wilson, Charles 132, 133
Wilson, Novella 149
Winter, John 37, 122, 126
Wirth, Mary 142
Wolf, Juanita 36
Wright, Leslie 75, 80
Wych, John G. 149
Wych, Norine 149, 179
Wyman, Martha 105

Y

Yunk, Troy 94, 151

ABOUT THE AUTHOR

Mike Doyle is a retired high school journalism teacher and former professional journalist who resides in Belvidere, Illinois. He is a member of the Boone County Historical Society. His first book was *April 21, 1967: The Belvidere Tornado*. This is the fifth book he has written or edited and his second for The History Press.